BASED ON A TRUE STORY

FROM PRISON TO PULPIT

From A Four Time Loser,
To A Lifetime Winner In Jesus Christ

BARBARA CAYWOOD

All scripture quotations, unless otherwise indicated, are taken from the *Holy Bible, King James Version. KJV.* Public Domain.

Cover design by Ryan Rogers. www.solaceillustrated.com

FIRST EDITION

ISBN: 9781936989089

Library of Congress Control Number: 2011926525

Published by
NewBookPublishing.com, a division of Reliance Media, Inc.
2395 Apopka Blvd., #200, Apopka, FL 32703
NewBookPublishing.com

Printed in the United States of America

DEDICATION

I dedicate this book to my wonderful husband. He lives his life to the fullest in Jesus Christ every day, everywhere he goes. He is an inspiration to me and encourages me daily to walk in faith and use my talents for the Lord. He is a blessing in my life and I thank God that he has put us together to serve in His kingdom side by side.

TABLE OF CONTENTS

He looked at the cocaine he had left. It was enough to do several more shots through the night and into tomorrow. I could put all of that dope into a syringe and shoot it all up. That would be more than enough to make me overdose and kill myself. I've seen people OD on less than half of that.

He mixed it with some water, drew it all up into a syringe, and shot it up. Within a few minutes he found himself slipping into utter darkness, sure he was on his way to death.

****

For the first time in his life he felt peace. He knew that God would be his everything, and that he wouldn't want for anything. He fell asleep with the Bible beside him, still basking in the presence of the Lord and the new experience of receiving the Holy Ghost.

FOREWORD

Rev. Kelly Caywood and his wife, Barbara have a special God-given gift of evangelism. Their passion for Jesus Christ is evident in their daily walk. This book is a wonderful testimony of how God can take a lost soul, turn his life around, and set his feet upon the solid rock for a lifetime of ministry.

Rev. Orlin W. McClain
Pastor Apostolic Temple,
Pasadena, TX

PREFACE

This book was written simply because God told me to. I wanted to have my wife write it from the different points of view, not just mine.

I truly believe that we are living in the last days. My hope and prayer is that this book finds its way into the hands of people that may not know God is real. God is truly not a respecter of persons. What He did for me, He can do for you. Whether it's drugs, alcohol, cutting yourself, or suicidal thought, there is but one answer - simply JESUS.

Kelly Caywood

Although I have heard my husband give his testimony numerous times, I never grow tired of hearing it. It is truly a miracle that he has made it through the drug addiction lifestyle to live a life in Jesus now. What astounds me, is that God didn't just deliver Kelly from the drugs, but He delivered him also from the whole lifestyle and way of thinking. When I see other addicts, I think, "That used to be my husband." I can't believe it. He is not the same man at all who he used to be.

Through the years we have had opportunities to work with people that have addictions. I did not live that lifestyle, so I do not have some of the same scars and cannot relate to them. But Kelly can. He is so transparent and real with them. Because he is real and is genuinely concerned for them, the stone walls that they have put up through the years to guard themselves start coming down. It is so amazing to see God working in their lives and the change take place. Everything they have lost all starts coming back, and then much more. God doesn't just bring you half way out, He brings you all the way out.

Barbara Caywood

ACKNOWLEDGEMENTS

I would like to thank my wife for all of her hard work, not only for this book, but also for me. She has allowed me to work through many issues and I am very thankful for that. Barbara is one of a kind, not only my wife, but also my best friend. Thank you, Babe, for believing in me when no one else would, and standing beside me through it all. I truly believe the best is yet to come.

Even though he has passed away, I owe a great thanks to Charles Mahaney. He came into my life at a time when I wasn't really sure if I would make it. I love you Brother Mahaney and miss you tremendously.

I thank Brother Nelson for loving me when I didn't even know how to love myself. He put up with a lot and loved me through it all. I love you, Bro. Nelson, and the church family there in Mont Belvieu, Texas.

Brother McClain has been such a God send to my wife and me. We came to him and Bishop McClain looking for guidance and leadership. What we have found surpassed our expectations and we now have a lifelong friendship. We love our pastor and church family in Pasadena, Texas.

To my mother who always believed in me and loved me

with tough love, I love you with all of my heart. You are the greatest. Thank you for never giving up on me. I love you, Mom.

Crystal and David, my beloved sister and brother, I love you both more than I could ever show or tell you. I believe in you tremendously.

Finally, my family whom I have become very close to after all of this, I love you and appreciate you all very much. Greg Rice, thank you for taking a chance on me. James, thank you for being like a dad to me. I love you both. To all of my aunts – I love you all, you guys are the greatest.

Kelly Caywood

PROLOGUE

1952 – Baytown, Texas

"Hi, Oma Lee. I wasn't expecting you," said Dorothy as she opened the door for her friend. Oma Lee lived down the road from Dorothy, so they were able to visit often, but usually Oma Lee called before she headed over.

Oma Lee walked into the house and carried the pie she held in her hands into the kitchen. "Well, I baked a couple of apple pies today for the kids. And I know how much you like my apple pies, so I thought I would bring one over. Wasn't any trouble to make an extra." Oma Lee was shorter than Dorothy, with dark, wavy hair, and she was always cooking and baking. It was one of her specialties, other than being a full-time mother to five girls. Since Oma Lee lived down the road from Dorothy, they were able to visit often.

"Thank you, that was nice of you. I'm always in the mood for one of your pies, no matter what kind it is."

Oma Lee smiled, knowing her cooking was always liked and appreciated. "You're welcome. Is your husband working this weekend?"

"Yes. Yours?"

"Yes. I hate it when they have to work weekends. But I guess we can't complain too much. At least they have a job, and Humble is a good company to work for."

"That is true. We're luckier than some."

Giving Dorothy a friendly squeeze on the shoulder, Oma Lee walked back toward the door. "Well, I can't stay long because I'm in the middle of cooking dinner, but I wanted you to have the pie before suppertime."

Dorothy was a little disappointed—it was lonely with her husband away. Trying to hide it, she said, "Oh, I wish we could visit, but I understand. Supper always calls." She lightened up, adding, "I've been meaning to ask you if Virginia could come watch Barbara next Thursday. I have a doctor's appointment."

"Yes. That will be fine. How old is Barbara now? I always forget."

"She's four," Dorothy said with a smile. "I forget too—it seems like just yesterday I was bringing her home from the hospital."

"Wow. They sure do grow up fast. Even though I have five girls, you never get used to how fast they grow up. Virginia just turned nine, and another grade higher in school. My, my." Oma Lee looked off in deep thought. "Well, I better get goin'. See ya later."

"Thanks again for the pie," Dorothy said as she saw Oma Lee out the door.

1965 – Champaign, Illinois

"Hey, Barbara, do you have Monday's notes?" asked Ashley, one of Barbara's classmates. "I missed all day of class."

"Why did you miss Monday? Still had a hangover from the weekend?"

"Something like that. They always said the University of Illinois was great academically, but whew, they never warned us about the parties," said Ashley exasperatedly.

"I hear ya there," Barbara said as she handed Ashley her notes from Monday. "Speaking of parties, don't forget about the party tomorrow at Jake's place."

"How could I forget! You've only been talking about it all week," Ashley said sarcastically.

"Well, at least I don't have to work this weekend."

"I've noticed you don't always make it to all of the parties. You still haven't told me where you work."

"Well, it's not something to brag about, but I am good at it," said Barbara, unsure if she should really tell Ashley her secret.

"Well?"

"I'm a high-paid prostitute." Barbara said it reluctantly in a gush of air, as if saying it in one breath would make it better. Getting her secret off her chest was oddly liberating, but scary, too.

Ashley was shocked. This beautiful, intelligent girl making money as a prostitute? She would have never thought it, but she could see how men would be attracted to Barbara— she was gorgeous and slender, and had inherited her mother Dorothy's dark hair, brown eyes, and olive skin. "*Wow*. What's the difference between a high-paid prostitute, and just a prostitute?"

Ashamed but proud, Barbara said, "I work different conventions. I work for the men with plenty of money. They are willing to pay good money if the work is good." Barbara now had a smirk on her face, as if she was better because of her ability.

Ashley, now sick to her stomach, said rather flippantly, "I guess if it makes you a living."

"Yeah, it does. A pretty good one."

Ashley got up from her desk, now ready to leave. "Thanks for Monday's notes. I'll see you in class for the test on Friday."

"You're welcome. And if you don't mind, could you keep what I just told you between us?"

"Yeah, sure."

"Thanks," Barbara said, as they both walked out of class. Just because she was proud of what she could do didn't mean she wanted to share it with everyone—they wouldn't understand. Plus, Barbara always needed more money than she had, and prostitution was an easy way to earn.

*****

"Hey, how's it going?" Barbara put on a fake smile and asked Ashley when she got to class. Two months had passed since Barbara had told Ashley what she did for a living, and that was not long after the fall semester had started. Now they just had polite conversation and went to parties together. Barbara wished she hadn't told Ashley about working as a prostitute, especially since she had met a new guy and quit her job soon after.

His name was William Daugherty, and he was tall, dark, and handsome. Barbara was totally infatuated with him. The only problem was, she had let her guard down with him. Now she was pregnant, and she knew it was his child. *What's he going to do when I tell him I'm pregnant? He's in the services, and living a free life. He's not going to want a child holding him down. What about me? What am I going to do with a child? I don't want a child to hold me down. My mother is going to kill me. What am I going to do?* These thoughts tormented her all day and night.

Barbara was deep in thought when Ashley answered her. "Pretty good. I've just been trying to keep up with all of these classes." Barbara still wasn't paying attention. "Hello! Is anyone home!"

Barbara snapped out of her thoughts and looked back at Ashley, "Oh, I'm sorry. I just have a lot on my mind." She then began to unload on Ashley and tell her the dilemma she had put herself in; despite the fact that their friendship hadn't been the same, Barbara needed someone to talk to. "Now it looks like I'm going to have to go back home, to Baytown, Texas, and face the consequences. I just don't know what to do. I don't want to drop out of school."

Ashley wasn't totally surprised Barbara had gotten pregnant, but she did feel a little sorry for her. "Well, now you can't just think about you. You have someone else to think about."

What am I going to do with a child? I don't want a child to hold me down.

"Yeah, I guess I do." Barbara knew that, but she didn't like it.

CHAPTER
~ *One* ~

1966 – Baytown, TX

"I'll see you when you get home this afternoon," Virginia said to Vernon as he walked out the door to go to the police academy. He had been in the police academy for only a short period of time; before that he had worked construction, but he had gotten tired of the sporadic nature of the work and was seeking a steady paycheck. Now he and Virginia had been married for five years, and although it had been a happy marriage so far, they still had not started a family. In fact, quite a few doctors had told Virginia she wasn't able to have kids, and therefore would never conceive. This grieved her, but she trusted in God. She knew that God would give her the desires of her heart if it was His will.

"Ok. See you later, sweetheart." He leaned back and gave her a quick peck on the cheek before hurrying out to his car.

Virginia spent the rest of the day cleaning house—a woman's job was never done, but it passed the time and she found fulfillment in all the small duties of running a home. As she prepared dinner that afternoon, she thought back to when she and Vernon had first gotten married. Oftentimes, Vernon would come home to a dinner of nothing more than scrambled eggs, with Virginia claiming not to be hungry. When he asked her why, she would say she had already eaten over at her mom's, where she could get a real, home-cooked meal. Those were the days.

Now, with some help from her mom, Virginia could whip up some good, hearty dinners all on her own. She laughed aloud at herself as she thought about it. *We would starve if I would've never learned how to cook.* On tonight's menu was fried chicken, real mashed potatoes, homemade cream gravy, and pinto beans.

Just as she was putting the last batch of chicken in to fry, the phone rang. "Oh, gatz. The phone always rings at the wrong time," Virginia said to herself as she wiped the flour from her hands and went to answer it.

"Hello?"

"Hey, are you sitting down?" It was her mom.

"No, I'm cooking dinner. What's wrong?"

"Nothing is wrong. You just need to be sitting down when I talk to you."

Virginia down on the couch. "Ok. I'm sitting down."

"Dorothy just called me. Barbara had a son a few months back, on the seventh of May. She got pregnant while she was going to college in Illinois. She isn't

> *Dorothy called me to see if you would be interested in having the baby.*

with the baby's father anymore, though. She's living with some guy by the last name of Caywood now. But neither one of them are responsible enough to keep a child. Dorothy called me to see if you would be interested in having the baby. She knows how bad you've always wanted a family, and she doesn't want to be raising a grandchild."

There was a long pause as Virginia soaked in all the information that her mother had just told her. It sure was a good thing she was sitting down.

"Are you sure?" Virginia said, a little doubtful.

"Yes, I am sure."

"What is the baby's name?"

"Samuel Douglas Caywood. He's only six months old."

Virginia still wasn't sure of everything. She had wanted a baby for so long, but didn't want to get her hopes up. With some restraint, she said, "I would love to have him, but I need to talk to Vernon first. I would also need some kind of papers. I would want it to all be legal, so that we're the rightful parents. Let me talk to Vernon. He'll be in any moment now, and then I'll call you back."

"Ok. I'll wait to hear from you before I call Dorothy back."

As Virginia continued working on dinner, barely saving the chicken from burning, her mind raced with all the thoughts of having a baby boy. *This would be a total miracle, especially knowing Dorothy and her family's background.* She had heard horror stories of some of the things they did and practiced. She knew that they would do séances with candles, and practice with tarot cards. The most gruesome was what she heard about the abortions. She had been told that they actually performed abortions, one time with a coat hanger, and would sometimes bury the fetuses in the back yard. Dorothy had always run around with all kinds of men, so of course she hadn't taught Barbara any better. The very thought of it all made Virginia cringe. The fact that Barbara hadn't had an abortion was a miracle in itself.

The more she thought about, the more she felt that God was giving her the baby she wanted, as well as giving the baby a chance at life—an opportunity for a loving, moral upbringing.

Of course, she still had fears of everything not going through. The fear of Barbara deciding to keep the baby. The fear of years down the road, if Barbara regretted what she had done and decided she wanted Samuel back. As the doubts flooded Virginia's mind, she knew that she had to understand that God was the One in control. And if she and Vernon were supposed to have the baby, then He would work it out.

When Vernon came in from the academy, he found Virginia deep in thought and more than a little distracted. "What's going on?" he asked.

Virginia, just realizing he was home, said, "A lot, but I'll talk to you about it over dinner."

Vernon sat his things down and went to get cleaned up as Virginia finished setting the table. When they finally sat down to eat, Virginia explained to Vernon everything that her mother had just told her.

There was a silence, and then Vernon said, "We would have to make it all legal—that's the only way I'll do it."

"I totally agree. And that's what I told mother."

"Then I say let's get him."

Virginia's heart swelled with joy—she was finally going to have the child she'd always wanted.

*****

Over the next couple of days, Virginia and Vernon experienced all the excitement that goes along with preparing for the arrival of a child. She took great pains to pick out the baby bed, clothes, food, and more. All the doubts Virginia had took a back seat to the joys of having a baby.

The custody papers didn't take long to receive. After reviewing their options, the couple realized that an actual adoption was costly and lengthy. But they could have legal custody of the baby, and this was all they needed to raise him as their own. Barbara was eighteen, and of legal age to sign

everything that was required of her. She had soon signed over all custody of Samuel.

As the day approached when they would pick up Samuel, there was much anticipation, but since Virginia had grown up knowing Dorothy and Barbara, it wasn't too difficult or awkward a transition. When Vernon and Virginia finally received Samuel, they were overjoyed. He looked like a little Indian baby. He had dark hair, big brown eyes, and his skin was dark complected. He was the most beautiful little baby boy Virginia had ever seen.

She couldn't stop smiling. On the way home, she said, "We left home as a family of two, and we are going home as a family of three."

Once home, they got Samuel settled in and got used to the idea of having a baby. They also talked about renaming him. Vernon said, "I would like for him to have our own last name, Downing."

"And I would like to choose his first name," put in Virginia.

As they all settled in, Virginia thought again about renaming him. They had thrown a couple of names around, but nothing seemed to fit. Then it was as if the light bulb went off in her head.

She turned to her husband, "Vernon, I know what we can name him. What about Stephen Kelly?"

Vernon thought about it for a moment, and then said, "I like it. I think it fits him. But we'll call him Kelly instead."

Virginia picked up the baby again and said, "Hey, Kelly. I'm momma, and I've loved you since I knew about you." While she played with Kelly she continued to talk to him.

Virginia and Vernon on Their Wedding Day

*****

As the weeks and months went on, Virginia and Vernon learned more and more about their baby boy. He was as happy a baby as ever. Oh, sure, he had his tantrum times, but he was more apt to scream and laugh than he was to scream and cry.

Virginia was glowing with her newfound motherhood—Kelly felt just as much her son as he would have if he had come from her own body. She was sitting on the floor one day and playing with Kelly, as she often did, giving thanks to God for this gift: *I would never have dreamed I could have this opportunity. To have a baby. A miracle baby.* The more she thought about it, she couldn't help but give God the glory, because she knew that neither she nor Vernon could've done this by themselves.

*****

When Kelly's one year birthday came, they planned a big party. All of their family and friends were happy for them, and the kitchen table was piled high with cake and presents. The Downings had only had Kelly for six months, but already they could not imagine life without this bundle of joy. He had just started walking, and they knew he would soon be running like all little boys. They cherished every moment, because they knew those moments would not be regained. The months seemed to pass in the blink of an eye.

*****

When Virginia walked through the door after returning from the store, she was met by a laughing, running toddler. Kelly was no longer that little baby who could barely crawl. He was now eighteen months old, and every bit a rough-and-tumble boy. He loved to run and climb on things like every little boy did, and was fascinated by trucks and animals.

Virginia's sister, Geneva, had been watching him while Virginia was out. Smiling a greeting, Virginia turned to Geneva and said, "Sometimes it seems like just yesterday we got him. It's hard to imagine that it's been a year now. They grow like weeds. He went from crawling, to walking, to running in no time. Next thing you know he'll be trying out for the football team and bringing home his first girlfriend."

Geneva laughed at her and said sarcastically, "Yep, they tend to be that way. They can't stay babies forever. By the way, Barbara called and said she would be running a little late."

Virginia sobered up when she remembered Barbara was coming. Barbara was allowed supervised visits with Kelly, as a condition of giving up legal guardianship. She also had another baby now, a little girl named Tasha. She was a newborn, but Barbara seemed to be doing okay with her so far. She normally didn't have Tasha with her, but today Dorothy couldn't babysit and so Barbara was bringing Tasha along.

Virginia always got nervous when Barbara was coming by. She never knew what Barbara was up to. She was so manipulative in everything she did that she could not be trusted in anything she said.

Virginia kept herself busy and visited with Geneva, trying to keep her mind off of the time when Barbara would come, and hoping she would make an excuse not to come at all. Twenty minutes later, though, a knock sounded at the door. Virginia's wish hadn't come true.

Barbara came in and made some small talk. She talked about anything and everything, as if she didn't want to stop for them to have time to think about anything.

"It looks like he has grown so much even since I last saw him," Barbara said, her tone exaggerated.

Virginia had butterflies in her stomach again. "It's only been two weeks since you last visited, and I doubt he's grown any in that time. Let me get some more toys here in the living room so you can play with him." As she went to get the toys, she made eye contact with Geneva. Her eyes sent a message to her sister that said, "Watch her! I don't trust her." And she didn't. Not one bit.

Everyone was sitting in the living room playing with Kelly when Virginia remembered she needed to start something for dinner. She excused herself and went into the kitchen, thankful that Geneva was there to help watch Barbara and Kelly. Virginia didn't like leaving them alone any more than she had to.

It's not that she thought anything would happen; it was just that she didn't trust Barbara. Wasn't that all she needed to feel nervous? Besides, it looked like Tasha had a little cold coming on, and she was fussy, so Barbara was having to concentrate a little more on her than on Kelly. It was good that Geneva was here to help with the children.

Virginia was in and out of the living room as she cooked dinner, and Barbara's interactions with Kelly didn't appear to be anything out of the ordinary. As the afternoon wore on, Barbara seemed to be a little more involved with Kelly than she had been earlier, and Geneva became more watchful. She didn't trust Barbara, either.

A few minutes later Geneva walked into the kitchen. "I don't feel all that comfortable in there by myself. Let me finish dinner and you can go watch them."

No one was in the room – no Barbara, no Kelly, and no Tasha.

Geneva's feelings made Virginia feel more apprehensive. "Is she acting any differently to make you feel this way?"

"Not really. It's just the way I feel. I don't know how to explain it."

Virginia talked to Geneva just a minute longer, told her what she was cooking, and then walked into the living room. What she saw when she got there was the shock of her life. No one was in the room—no Barbara, no Kelly, and no Tasha. Virginia stood there in shock for a minute before she screamed for Geneva. When Geneva rushed into the room, Virginia ran outside. No one was there. Barbara's car was gone.

She cried out, "Oh, God, watch over my baby! I know that crazy woman has him. Please bring him back to me." Virginia continued to cry out and pray to God. She felt like she had no control, but she knew the One who did, and she prayed for Him to help her.

Geneva had jumped into action while Virginia sat crying. She called Vernon, who could not believe what he was hearing. Then he reported the kidnapping to the police, and rushed to a home that now felt empty.

CHAPTER
~ *Two* ~

Barbara hadn't thought she was actually going to be able to get little Samuel. (They may have renamed him, but he was still Samuel to her.) She had never wanted to give him up in the first place— her parents had made her. *Who cares if I may not be the most responsible person, he's my son! No one can take care of him as good as I can*, she thought. *I should never have let my parents force me into giving him up.* When Virginia and Geneva had left her alone with Samuel, she had seen the opportunity and taken it.

Barbara was no longer with her most recent boyfriend, Craig Caywood. He just wasn't her type anymore. Instead, she had turned to her ex-boyfriend, Charles. He always gave her whatever she wanted anyway. She knew she could work him, and that he would be like putty in her hands. He didn't have to know she had two babies right off. All he had to know was that she left Craig for him. That alone would make him feel good. Not to mention the fact that he thought she was dropping everything and running to him in Dallas.

She wasn't lying to him about her kids; she just

hadn't told him yet. Had Charles known that she was bringing "extra baggage" with her, he may have thought she was an inconvenience. But right now, she didn't know who else to turn to. Her parents didn't want her to have one baby, much less two. Neither did anyone else in her family. Hopefully he would warm up to the babies once he saw that she was coming back to him.

The sad part was that Barbara herself wasn't even sure if she wanted two babies. She just felt guilty for giving Samuel up in the first place. Through all the emotional struggles over the last year, she had finally made a choice to get Samuel back. That final choice came with the birth of her baby girl. The feel of Tasha in her arms made her long for Samuel again. It made her wonder how big he was, what his smile was like, and what his favorite toys were.

Lying in the hospital bed, she had made up her mind to get him back. It took a while to come up with a plan. She knew she couldn't just go to the Downings and demand him back— they had legal rights to him and would never give him up. She would have to kidnap her own son. How chaotic did that sound! Kidnapping her own son! He was *her* son, and he belonged to *her*. Not with some other woman. The more she thought about it, the angrier she became. She blamed everyone for the pain she had been through, never realizing the consequences of her own actions.

But now she had Samuel, and she had a plan. She was headed to Dallas and leaving everyone else behind. She was torn between keeping the lifestyle she had, and being a mom. It wasn't that she had to have Samuel with her all the time— she just wanted to be "momma" to him. Not for Virginia to be "momma." Whenever she heard those words coming from Samuel's sweet baby mouth, it hurt her heart. When she was lonely, she loved that feeling that only a baby could give. That sense of belonging to someone, even if it was a child. That sense that she was needed, and loved in return. Somehow, she would figure out a way to keep her lifestyle and her kids.

*****

Vernon came home to a still-frantic Virginia, who was relentlessly beating herself up for not staying in the room with Barbara. Then Geneva started feeling bad, apologizing for walking out of the living room in the first place.

After Vernon got the ladies calmed down, he tried to talk to them in a level-headed fashion. "This is no one's fault but Barbara's," he said calmly. "No one knew Barbara was going to leave with Kelly—she hasn't ever shown any indication that she wanted him back. Ya'll couldn't have known."

The two women finally pulled themselves together. Vernon had told them the Baytown Police Department was coming by and that they give the authorities a full report. The sooner they made the report, the sooner Kelly would be returned to them.

When they got to the police arrived, they reported everything they knew. Since Barbara never had a place where she stayed for long periods of time, the police said it would be a little more difficult to find her. They didn't offer much hope, but said they would put out the search.

Virginia left discouraged, not knowing what to do and feeling like her hands were tied. She couldn't sleep that night and was a wreck all day; the house was filled with memories of Kelly, and she couldn't be sure that Barbara was taking care of him as he should be taken care of.

Girl Has Never Used An Alias, Relatives Say

Mrs. Barbara Caywood, 19, sought by Baytown police on a charge of kidnapping, has never used an alias, according to her grandmother.

Mrs. K. E. Martin of 6612 Steinman said her granddaughter has never used any name but her maiden name, Martin, and married name, Caywood.

Mrs. Caywood is charged with kidnapping her 15-month-old son. Police allege legal custody of the child had been granted to Mrs. Virginia Downing of 3202 Michigan.

Previous reports of the kidnapping charge quoted police reports stating that Mrs. Caywood had been known to use last-name aliases of Martin, Clements and McKinney.

Relatives, however, say this is not true.

Authorities said Monday morning Mrs. Caywood is still at large.

The Baytown Sun Newspaper Article

The next day when Vernon got home he sat Virginia down. "I'm going to use our savings to hire a private investigator. He will look harder for Kelly than the police will because he's getting paid."

"Whatever it takes," Virginia said before she broke down in tears. "I just want my son back."

*****

Barbara had made it to Dallas, but the welcome from Charles wasn't as warm as she had hoped it would be. He didn't like kids, and didn't even take care of his own. He only wanted Barbara because she was cute and fun, not because he loved her or wanted to take care of her. He would compromise in the beginning some, but not much. He wasn't sure who would keep her bratty kids while they partied, but he had to have her on his arm when he went out. It didn't help that Samuel cried constantly. He would throw tantrums and fuss until he almost made himself sick. Barbara was having a hard time dealing with him and Tasha, who was still a newborn and required a lot of attention. It was nine o'clock, and both kids were still awake. *Ugh, life was easier when I didn't have kids. I wish I knew someone I could drop them off with. I love 'em and all, but, whew, all the time with them. It's just too much. It has only been a week and a half, and I am having a hard time. I need to go to a party and have a few beers. That would help take some stress off.*

As if reading her mind, Charles walked in. "Hey, do you want to go out tonight? I just want to go have a good time with you like we used to."

"Oh, you don't know how I wish we could, but I don't have anyone to keep the kids," she answered.

"What about Tammy? She's good with kids. I am sure she would. I could ask her for you."

Tammy was a friend of theirs who had taken a liking to Tasha and Samuel. "That would be great if she could. Samuel is getting on my last nerve."

As Charles went to make the phone call, Barbara started getting some things together for the kids. She just knew Tammy would say yes, and she welcomed the night off. Charles came back and asked, "Are you ready? She said she would keep them."

Excited, Barbara hurried and finished up. She was getting the night off!

*****

It had been two months since Kelly had been kidnapped. The police and the private investigator had followed every lead they received, but nothing came up. There had even been a newspaper ad in the Baytown Sun where the police were trying to find Barbara under different aliases, but all their tips had turned to dead ends. Virginia and Vernon checked with the private investigator and the Baytown Police Department every day, and each day without progress in finding Kelly left them feeling more and more discouraged.

Virginia, now alone in their house every day, was having a hard time until Vernon came home excited one afternoon. He met Virginia in the kitchen cooking dinner, his face hopeful. "We have a lead! The private investigator called and said they got a tip saying Barbara is in Illinois, where Kelly's biological father is from. They have someone up there they're going to send to follow-up on the lead, but I think we should go up there ourselves and see what we can find out."

He didn't have to say another word—Virginia was ready

to go as soon as she heard him say "We have a lead." "When can we leave?" she asked impatiently.

"Tomorrow."

It took two days to get to Illinois. They followed up on the lead, which led to another lead, which led to another lead, which led to a dead end. When they returned home a week later, almost depleted of savings, they were exhausted and discouraged. Nothing had turned up, and they were almost out of money. When their savings were gone, they would no longer be able to keep looking for their lost son.

Now as Virginia sat at home, she wondered if she would ever see Kelly again. After two months of not having him, she was beginning to lose hope. Not knowing what else to do, she turned the whole situation over

We have a lead.

to God. She knew that He had all things in control, even when the situation looked bleak. All she knew to do now was pray. Pray for herself, to keep her sanity, and pray for Kelly, that he was safe and happy. She just knew that wherever he may be, the situation couldn't be good. As she encouraged herself in the Lord, she went on about unpacking from the long week.

*****

Barbara looked at her two babies and gave them one last hug. It was March, and the news had come to her yesterday that the police and a private investigator were on her trail. After talking to Charles and Tammy, she decided for Tammy to keep the kids while she and Charles went somewhere else to live for a little while until the situation settled down. At least once all the commotion died off, she could see her kids again. Although, she had to admit, she sure liked the freedom of being able to come and go as she pleased. Tammy always agreed to watch the kids so Barbara could go party. Tammy didn't take care of the kids as well as Barbara would have liked, but it was free, and Barbara knew where they were and could get them any time she wanted.

But for now, she had to leave Tasha and Samuel. She couldn't risk being caught by the police and going to jail. The very thought of it scared her to death. And then what would happen to her kids? As Barbara left the house without much longing for the kids at the moment, she didn't realize what the future held. In her naïve mind, she thought she would leave for a few months, then return to see the kids again, and then continue to party and come and go.

Life here with Charles was good. She got to see her kids often, had someone to help take care of them, and she got to party. Both were things she wanted, and both were things she got. What she never stopped to realize was that her lifestyle choices held consequences, some life-long.

*****

Tammy was so glad when Barbara and Charles left. She was jealous of Barbara. She had always liked Charles, but never said anything. She hated seeing them together. She was being used by both of them and knew it. Tammy knew that if she did whatever Charles wanted, even if it meant she had to endure some things she didn't want to, that he would come running to her, because she was always there for him. He would eventually see that no one else would love him or take care of him like she would.

Tammy didn't care about Barbara's kids at all—they had merely been a way to get closer to Charles, to show her worth to him. Now that Barbara would be gone for a while, Tammy could treat the kids however she wanted. There was no compassion in Tammy whatsoever, especially for Charles' girlfriend's kids. Who else to take her jealousy of Barbara out on, except for the children?

*****

Virginia had a fun day out with her sisters shopping—it had been too long since they had a sisters' day. It helped take her mind off of things for a short time, and they had encouraged her to keep up her hope and her spirits, just as they always did. Virginia wasn't sure what she would have done without their support in this hard time. While unpacking her purchases from the day, she got a phone call.

"Hello?"

"Hi, may I speak with Mrs. or Mr. Downing please?"

"This is Virginia Downing."

"This is Edward Smith, and I'm a lawyer here in Dallas. We have found your son, Samuel, who you call Kelly."

Virginia didn't know whether laugh, scream, cry, or do all three. She sat down on the couch and took the information in. After six months, they had finally found him. And all this time he was in Dallas, only four hours away. After a moment, she realized the lawyer had never said how Kelly was doing. "Is he okay?" she asked. "Is my son okay?"

"Well...." The lawyer hesitated a minute, knowing the words would be a harsh reality, but he couldn't lie either. "He hasn't been taken care of as a child should be."

He paused as he heard Virginia take her breath in and give a whimper, as if she had already started crying. It was hard for him to finish telling her everything. "He has bruises all over him, and a few cigarette burn marks. His hair is long, like it hasn't been cut in a while. He shies away from everyone, like he is scared."

Virginia sat with tears rolling down her face. She had known it might be bad, but she had never thought it would be this bad. "Where did you find him? Where is Barbara?" she asked, her anger toward Barbara growing. She didn't understand why Barbara had taken a child she wasn't even interested in caring for.

He has bruises all over him, and a few cigarette burn marks.

"We found him in Barbara's boyfriend house with another lady watching them. Barbara is now in jail. When we captured her, she finally told us where Kelly was. There were a lot of kids there, including his little sister, Tasha. Now, I know you and your husband have custody of Kelly, but do you also want custody of Tasha? Because I can tell you now, Barbara will not be regaining custody of her kids. She is not fit to be a mother, especially after leaving the kids in that environment."

Virginia knew they couldn't afford another child. They had already spent everything they had searching for Kelly. "I am sorry, but we can't. We really can't afford to take care of another baby. I will try to think of someone who may be able to take her, though. My main concern is for my son."

"I understand, Mrs. Downing. I wanted to offer Tasha to you first to try to keep brother and sister together. I have also considered taking her myself. And now, since you cannot keep her, I will. She will not be going back to her mother."

After Virginia talked to him a little longer and got his phone number and address, she went straight to the police academy to tell Vernon. He left with her, and they went home to get things together, then headed north on I-45 to Dallas. Virginia was full of anticipation and sorrow. She didn't know exactly what sight she was going to see when she got to Kelly—she just knew she wanted to hold him, to show him that he was safe and loved. No matter what had happened, they would get through it together.

When Virginia and Vernon got to Dallas, Kelly was not the same little boy who had left six months earlier. He shied away from them a little at first, and when he finally came to them, he was still a little distant. He had long hair, bruises, and cigarette burn marks, and was dirty from head to toe. Virginia wanted to cry over the way he looked, and she could only imagine what state he was in emotionally. He had already been through so much for a child only two years old.

After they got home, they got a phone call from the lawyer about what happened with Barbara. The judge would not grant her custody of her kids, and had said that she was not fit to be a mother. He also said she should be happy her kids were in good homes. The judge figured she wouldn't have to serve much jail time, because having her kids taken away was enough to get her attention and put her on a better path. The lawyer was going to keep Tasha, and the Downings were going to keep Samuel.

*****

For the next few months, things were tough. Kelly would stand in a corner often, as if he was scared of everyone. He wasn't the happy little boy he once had been. That big smile and shining eyes were gone, and in their place was a dull, frightened look. He didn't trust anyone. He would flinch when a hand was raised around him.

After much prayer and love, the son they once knew finally started to come back around. He started playing more, and laughing more. He even started talking more.

Virginia knew that God had given her this little miracle, and that He would keep him and make him happy and well.

CHAPTER
~ *Three* ~

As Kelly grew older, he became a big brother. Virginia was blessed with two more children, Crystal and David. It turned out the doctors had been wrong, and Virginia's faith in God was rewarded. Kelly and his siblings were a few years apart, but the two younger children adored their older brother. He was always full of mischief, and the days were never boring when Kelly was around.

Crystal was a healthy, rambunctious little girl, taking after her older brother, of course. She was always full of ideas and energy.

David was premature and had meningitis as a baby. Although he was a little slow, he was always a good sport, which served to Kelly and Crystal's advantage. David was the poor little brother that got all the pranks pulled on him. One day Virginia came home and found David in the dryer. When she asked Kelly and Crystal why he was in the dryer, their response was, "Because we couldn't fit him in the washing machine."

Another time when Virginia came home, she found David duct taped to a chair with Vernon's handcuffs on. Crystal and Kelly were trying to saw the handcuffs off. Virginia could not believe her eyes. *What have they gone and done now?* She asked herself. She knew Vernon was the only one who had the key, and being a police officer, he wouldn't leave the keys with the handcuffs. She finally got the duct tape cut away from David, but he would have to wait until his dad got home for the handcuffs to come off. And Vernon would not be happy at all.

As the children's' pranks grew, so did their enemies. Another time, after days of not receiving the mail, Virginia flagged down the mail lady and asked her why she wasn't getting her letters any more. The mail lady replied angrily, "Ask your children! Maybe you should pay attention to what they do!"

When she asked the kids if they knew why she wasn't getting any mail, they began to roll on the floor laughing. After getting them to quiet down, Virginia scolded, "One of you better answer me, or you're all getting punished."

Kelly finally spoke up in defense. "We were just having fun. At least no one got hurt this time."

Virginia questioned again, "What did you do?"

"Well, we gave the mail lady a brown paper bag and told her we made her lunch," Kelly said as a smile crept across his face, "but we really had a plastic snake in the bag." Then he rolled on the floor again laughing. "She said, 'Well, thank you. How sweet of you!' And when she got a couple of houses down we heard her scream and we took off running into the house." He continued laughing. "It was our best prank ever." By this time all the siblings were laughing. Needless to say, Virginia did a lot of apologizing to the mail lady, but it still took her a week to start getting her mail again.

Virginia, Kelly, and Crystal

Kelly at 7 Years Old

*****

However, not all was harmonious in the Downing home. Kelly slowly realized that there was a change in his dad. The man who used to go to church and loved the Lord had walked out on God and was growing more bitter and sarcastic every day. There was no more compassion in Vernon, and not much love either. He was continuously putting Virginia and the kids down. Whatever he thought of that was sarcastic and might hurt a little, he said. Never did he realize the lasting effects his harsh words would have on his children. But when someone gets bitter at God, they tend to take that anger out on everyone, even the ones they are supposed to love.

Virginia and Vernon had never told Kelly he was adopted and had decided to keep it a secret, just like he was their own blood. However, Vernon didn't always act like Kelly was his own child. Oftentimes, he would leave Kelly out and only do things with Crystal and David. Crystal would try her best to include Kelly in these fun times with their dad, but she wasn't always successful, and Vernon didn't realize what he was doing emotionally to Kelly by leaving him out of the fun.

Virginia, being a mom, always tried to be the peacemaker. Even when she told Vernon what he was doing, he ignored her and told her that she was making his treatment of Kelly out to be more than it was. That he wasn't leaving Kelly out. That she just tried too hard to make Kelly feel a part of the family.

As a child, the isolation from Vernon didn't have much of an effect on Kelly. He made good grades in school, was very popular, and was very athletic. Other than his mischievousness, he was a good, smart kid. He went to church with his other siblings and mom and excelled in anything he did. It wasn't until he was eleven years old that his whole world changed.

*****

Virginia was so glad to be home from work and off of her feet for a few minutes before starting on supper. She was doing what she was trained to do, but it could be exhausting. She was a nurse, and a good one. She had put herself through college while Vernon was working as a police officer at the Baytown Police Department. No one had ever told her how expensive it would be to raise three kids. It took both her and Vernon working to provide for them.

As Virginia savored her few moments off of her feet, the phone rang. Virginia answered it. "Hello?"

It was her mom, Oma Lee. "Hey, I just heard some bad news. Barbara is back in town."

There was a long silence while Virginia thought about what she had just been told. She had that uneasy feeling that something was going to be wrong. "If you say it's bad news and she's back in town, then that must mean something. What else did you hear?"

> *Hey, I just heard some bad news. Barbara is back in town.*

Oma Lee let out a breath. "She wants to see Kelly. She's on a rampage telling everyone she wants to see her son. And she's calling you all kinds of names that I am not going to repeat. She can't be trusted, Virginia. Just be careful. I don't even know if Kelly should stay there. She knows where you live. Maybe he should go stay somewhere else until she leaves again, or until you run into her, or something. I don't know. I just don't like the situation at all."

Virginia felt frantic. "I can't just let Kelly go stay somewhere. He'll want to know why. Then that will mean I have to tell him the truth. I don't know if I can do that. It would be too hard." Just the thought of having to tell Kelly the truth about being adopted made her feel sick. He was already having a hard enough time dealing with how emotionally distant Vernon was. "I have to go and think about this. I'll have to talk to Vernon. I don't know what we'll do."

As she hung up the phone, she knew the inevitable was going to happen. The day she had dreaded since she first brought Kelly home was coming. She had hoped that she would never have to tell him, but Barbara wouldn't let that happen. She would do whatever she could to make their lives miserable. Virginia was barely able to cook supper because of the emotions that were raging inside of her. When Vernon got home, the three of them would have to talk.

It was late when Vernon finally walked through the front door. The kids had already eaten and were playing in their bedroom. Vernon knew something was wrong by Virginia's unusual silence, but instead of asking and encouraging her, he decided to nag her. He said sarcastically, "Let me guess, you're gonna complain that your feet hurt, and all you want to do is put your p.j.'s on and go to bed. Yeah, then just complain. You act like you're the only one who works around here. What's for supper? I'm starvin'."

Virginia gave him a drop dead look. "Yes, my feet do hurt, but I wasn't going to complain. And yes, sometimes I feel like I am the only one who works, because my job isn't done when I get home. And fried chicken and mashed potatoes are for supper. Happy?"

"Oh well, whoopdy-do. I'm only happy if Kelly didn't eat all of the chicken and mashed potatoes. Did you make biscuits? If you did, I bet he ate all of them too. I swear, that boy eats everything in this house."

As he complained about Kelly eating, all Virginia could do was cringe. Kelly was a growing boy. He was tall and skinny, and he needed to eat to put some meat on his bones. Oh, but if Vernon only knew about what they were getting ready to face! Well, it wouldn't matter. He would still be sarcastic and complain about everything.

"I'll fix your plate, and then we need to talk."

"Oh, what happened at work that's so bad? Who are they talking about now?"

Virginia wasn't in the mood for his sarcasm, not after all of the emotions that she had already gone through tonight. She raised her voice. "Vernon, dead gummit, I am being serious now. Stop messing around."

He looked like a little kid who was told to stop playing. He got quiet and started eating. "Well then, what's so serious?"

"Mom called today."

"Okay? She calls every day."

Virginia tolerated his sarcasm and continued. "She said that Barbara is back in town." This got his attention. "That Barbara was telling everyone she wants to see her son. She is calling me all kinds of names, and…" she paused and threw her hands up in the air in exasperation, "she's just going berserk."

They sat in silence for a minute. Then Vernon said, "You know what we're going to have to do, don't you?"

"Yes, my worst nightmare." Though she had thought about it for the last couple of hours, actually voicing it made her fears even greater. She couldn't contain the tears that had been threatening her all evening. She began to cry. She knew deep down that this would be the first of many tears that would be shed. The hardest part was still to come. "Mom suggested that Kelly leave for a little while. I'm leaning toward agreeing with her. I'm just not sure what Barbara is going to try to do."

Vernon thought for a minute, "Yeah, we'll have to send him somewhere, at least for a week. Just until things die down some. We can send him to one of your sisters. Which one?"

"The only one who doesn't have anything going on right now and could really help watch him, for his own safety, is Brenda. He could go to Brenda and Dave's house for a week."

When Vernon finished eating, he called to Kelly to come to the living room.

Kelly came in. "Yeah, Dad?"

"Sit down on the couch, son, we need to talk to you."

"Whatever it was, I swear it wasn't me. I haven't pulled any pranks in two weeks. And then, I just shot at Crystal with a BB gun while she held a cardboard box. She only has a couple of bruises, she's not hurt. I promise." He was earnestly defending himself, especially since he was always the one getting into trouble for his little schemes.

"You shouldn't have been shooting at your sister with a BB gun, but that's not what I have to talk to you about. I am being serious now, boy."

Kelly sobered up and waited for Vernon to speak. He could see Virginia was on the verge of tears. *Whatever I did this time made them really mad. But Dad doesn't look mad. Why is Mom starting to cry? I've really been trying to do better. I just get bored, and they don't understand. What else am I supposed to do?*

"We have never told you this before because we didn't want to hurt you," Vernon said, before pausing for what seemed like an eternity.

Okay, this is not what I thought it was going to be. What's going on? Kelly's thoughts were going a mile a minute.

Vernon continued, "I don't know any way to sugar coat this, or make it sound better. So I'm going to just come out and say it. We are not your real mom and dad. We adopted you when you were six months old. Your real mom is back in town and wants to see you." All he could hear was Virginia's soft sobbing as he waited for some kind of response from Kelly.

We adopted you when you were six months old.

Kelly just had a blank stare, as if he'd gotten the wind knocked out of him and couldn't find his next breath.

"She has already kidnapped you once, back when you were fifteen months old. She had you for six months before we found you, and she didn't treat you right. It isn't safe for you to be here right now. You're going to have to go stay with your Aunt Brenda for at least a week."

Stunned, Kelly looked at his mom and dad, as if seeing them for the first time. Everything he had known was a lie. He had always known he was different, but he had never understood how or why. Now he knew. Virginia and Vernon weren't his real parents. They had lied to him all of these years. They had only pretended. He knew they didn't really love him. This must be why Vernon treated him differently than he treated Crystal and David.

Kelly at 11 Years Old

Now that Kelly knew the truth, he felt he was on his own. His parents had no say so over him. He could be his own boss, because they had no control. The stunned reality quickly became bitterness. He said very angrily and with a cocky attitude, "Well, if you're not my parents, then you can't tell me what to do. And if you can't tell me what to do, then I'm outta here." Then he ran out of the room and into his bedroom, slamming the door shut behind him.

Neither Virginia nor Vernon ran after him. They didn't know what exactly to expect, but they knew it wasn't going to be pretty. Vernon went on about his business, because he was always numb and sarcastic anyway. His way of dealing with things was to say harsh words and withdraw from his family. There wasn't anything he could say that would make things better. He would probably just make them worse.

Virginia sat silently and wept. She felt helpless, because she really didn't know what to say. She realized you're not always prepared for what life brings you, and you don't always know how to deal with it. After a few hours, she started to read a book, her escape from reality.

She would leave Kelly alone and let him work through his emotions. Once he wasn't angry anymore, she would be able to talk to him. Then he would go to Brenda's tomorrow.

CHAPTER
~ *Four* ~

Barbara never ended up posing a threat to them as they had originally thought. She never showed up, and Kelly went unharmed, other than the truth he now carried. What was said could never be unsaid, and the damage done to his emotions could never be undone. Virginia didn't know if Kelly would ever forgive her and love her like a son is supposed to love his mother, because he no longer felt like she was his mother.

Over the next several months Kelly's grades began to drop. He had always been a good student with very good grades, as well as one of the school's best athletes. Talent scouts were already looking at him for college scholarships. They thought that if he was so skilled at sports at his age, he would only get better.

Kelly used to care about all of that. He had been a real go-getter. But now everything he used to excel at was quickly deteriorating. Now all he had inside was bitterness and hatred. Once an extremely outgoing kid, he was now a little more quiet and reserved. He didn't talk to his friends that often. He was isolating himself from them.

He eventually dropped his long-time friends and began hanging with a different group of kids—the kind of kids you would never want your children to hang out with. They had mischievousness like Kelly did, but in a much more negative way. His new friends, coupled with his bitterness, turned into deeper rebellion than Virginia could ever have imagined. He was strong-willed and hard-headed. If you told him not to do something, he would do it just for spite. This once fun-loving, caring pre-teen slowly moved more into himself and became more troublesome.

*****

Riding the bus on his way home from school, Kelly was deep in thought over the last couple of months. *I never liked going to church. I don't believe in the Holy Ghost and all of that baptism in Jesus' name stuff anyway. None of that is real. They just faked it. What does it matter that I pull some really mean pranks now? No one can tell me what to do. Besides, Dad used to go to church, and it didn't help him any. Or do I call him Dad? Whoever he is, he's mean. He doesn't like anybody, especially me. Church didn't help him, so why should it help me? No one understands me. And they never will. That's why it's all about me now. Forget church.*

Kelly didn't realize another boy named Scott was trying to get his attention just as they were all getting off of the school bus. "Hey, Kelly, where are you, in outer space or somethin'? Why don't you come down to earth where real people live?"

Did Scott just say what I thought he said? Is he trying to make fun of me and embarrass me? He is going to wish he never did that! I am going to make an example out of him, and then all the other kids will know not to mess with me.

As Kelly came off of the bus, he dropped his back pack to the ground and began beating up Scott, taking out all of his anger on him. Kelly was blinded by the anger that was fuming inside of him. The only thing he could think about was hurting Scott, and that maybe it would make him feel better inside. He was on top of the boy, pummeling his face and chest.

Some of the other kids were surrounding them and shouting, "Fight! Fight! Fight!" But it was a distant roar to Kelly's ears.

"Get him, Kelly!"

"Get up, Scott! Punch him back!"

Before some of the other kids were able to pull Kelly off, Scott had a swollen and bruised face, a bloody nose, and a busted lip.

After some name calling, Scott went home crying.

Kelly went home with anger still in him.

*****

Kelly's new "friends" weren't the greatest, but at least they were more like him than the other kids he used to hang with, and he would much rather spend time with them than at home. They had also introduced him to marijuana. It numbed the pain inside of him for a short time, and though its effects never lasted long enough, at least he could enjoy life for a little while.

Kelly walked in the front door to the smell of dinner cooking. *I guess Mom got off work early today.* He tried to get to his room without her saying anything. The less that was said the better. *I'm really not angry at her anymore—besides, she's the only mom I know. Now, Dad, or Vernon...I don't know if there will ever be anything there.*

Virginia tried to force a smile when she saw the torment

across Kelly's face. If she knew her son, he wanted to show love, but was too proud to do so. "Hey, we were slow at work today so I got to come home early. I've got chicken fried steak cooking. You're favorite," she said with excitement.

"Great. Thanks, Mom. Let me know when it's ready," he said in a dry tone and without so much as a glance in her direction went straight to his room. It felt better to stay mad, rather than to be glad and then just get disappointed again.

> *When Kelly got to his room he went to his trashcan, took out the bag of trash, got some pot out,...*

As hard as Virginia tried, she never could get through to Kelly. He had built up so many walls around him that there was no penetrating them. She knew he was angry and depressed and bitter, but she didn't know how to reach him. He was still her son, but it was like she didn't know him anymore. She remembered the sweet, affectionate child he had once been, and it made her heart hurt.

Every day Kelly came home, ate, and left to go hang out with friends. Then he would come home just in time for bed. *I know his friends are different now, and I don't know the new ones that well, but they're all pre-teens. What influence could they possibly have on Kelly?* Virginia asked herself.

When Kelly got to his room he went to his trashcan, took out the bag of trash, got some pot out, and opened his bedroom window so he could smoke. He turned his radio on and turned it up, though not loud enough to make Virginia fuss, and just chilled.

It wasn't long before Virginia was calling him for dinner, but Kelly wasn't able to get his plate and go back to his room without talking to his father, who was sitting on the couch, watching television. When Kelly went to put his plate in the kitchen sink Vernon said, "Can't find nothin' better to do than hole up in your room? Grass needs cuttin'. Leaves need rakin'. There's all kinds of things you could be doing to be productive with your time, son."

"You're not doing anything right now. Why don't you get up and do something?" With anger boiling, Kelly snapped, "And don't call me son, I am not your son! You're not my dad!" Then he stormed out of the house.

Virginia didn't see that there was anything she could do, so she went back in the kitchen to clean up. *At least dishes don't argue.*

Vernon went back to watching the television as if nothing had happened—and by now their daily arguments were the usual scene anyway, not new anymore. Kelly went to Jake's house, but after getting there realized he didn't want to just sit around. He needed to get outside and walk off some anger and energy. While out walking around the neighborhood, the two boys came across a coke machine, and Jake decided he was thirsty. Together they tried to break into it and take some cokes; it never crossed their minds to take the money.

They got the cokes, but they didn't enjoy their success for long. A cop had been watching them from around the corner the whole time, and he showed no mercy. He took them down to the Baytown Police Department and pinned a robbery on them. There was fear inside of them, but they were too proud to show it.

The police officer escorted each one of the boys home and spoke with their parents. When he took Kelly home, Virginia held up a good front at first, but it didn't last long. She broke down crying once the officer left. Kelly tried to apologize, but it didn't do any good. Virginia knew there would be consequences, but Kelly didn't quite understand.

However, Kelly soon came to a fast understanding of what his actions would do. The judge ordered him to the Harris County Youth Village in Clearlake, Texas, for six months. Virginia was torn between wanting to discipline Kelly and wanting to hold him for a long time, long enough to take away the pain and anger she knew was building inside of him.

He was too young to be experiencing these strong emotions. But she felt helpless, and all she knew to do was to pray. There was no manual or quick answer to parenting. Vernon was just as angry as Kelly, and they fed off of each other. Kelly's breaking into the coke machine had just pushed him and Vernon further apart.

The day came when Virginia had to take Kelly to the Youth Village. She cried that morning, but tried to take solace in believing that the Village would help turn around some of the rebellion that was inside of Kelly. They made small talk on the way, but he mostly remained quiet. That was the new him, either angry or quiet.

Kelly was scared; after all he was eleven years old and going to jail! But he didn't let on that he was scared. He was good at hiding his emotions behind a stone face. He didn't know what he would face when he got there, how many fights he would get in, or the kind of food he would eat. He just knew he was ready for it to be over.

Despite his trepidation, Kelly quickly got into a monotonous routine. Disgusting food, boring school, and sleepless nights. There was a little time for recreation, but not much. The kids there were of all different ages, and Kelly learned a whole lot more than just the basic educational subjects while he was there. He learned some more tricks, manipulation tactics, and how to work the system.

Virginia was good about visiting him often and bringing him pies from home. He had lost some weight while at the camp, but he always looked forward to his mom's homemade pies.

By the end of the six weeks, Kelly's heart was harder than it had been before. However, he couldn't hide his excitement at being able to come home and not having to stay another night at the Harris County Youth Village.

CHAPTER
~ *Five* ~

O ver the next few years, Kelly didn't find enjoyment in much of anything except for smoking marijuana and cigarettes, drinking alcohol, and taking mandrex pills. At some point he had fallen out of touch with what normal feelings and normal thinking were. In his mind and his world, it was a haze of pain and anger. When he went to church with his mom, he would moan and complain the whole time. His heart was so calloused, even at such a young age, that he never even responded to the moving of the spirit of God.

Try as she may, Virginia couldn't get through to Kelly. After a while she began to grow tired of fighting him about staying out all night. She would smell different drugs on him but never knew what they were, and he would lie to her when she questioned him about what he was doing and where he had been. It was sometimes easier for her to ignore his misbehaviors or to be in denial and believe that he was a good kid who was just going through a phase.

It was even worse when Kelly and Vernon would get into arguments. Vernon never would relent on Kelly. He had to stoop to name calling and picking on Kelly as if they were the same age, rather than father and son. Vernon favored Crystal and David over Kelly, but that didn't mean he was any nicer to them. It seemed none of the kids could escape his verbal harassment.

Kelly was always at one party or another, even if most of the people there were older than him. He knew he had a better chance of getting the smokes, dope, alcohol, and pills around older kids, and at that point in his life, drugs and drinking were all he did. He knew there were other, heavier drugs, but he could never get his hands on those, because they cost a lot of money. So far, he was able to sell some marijuana, make a little money, and get what he could.

Trevor was one of the older guys who came occasionally to the same parties that Kelly attended. He had been watching Kelly for a little while and knew that Kelly was ready for some harder stuff. One night at a party he pulled Kelly to the side and said, "Hey, buddy, I know you like that pot and all, but I got something I think you would like better."

Kelly was willing to try anything. Nothing was out of the question for him. "Yeah, this stuff is good, but if you have something better I'll try it."

"Stick out your arm. You're gonna feel a little prick, but it won't hurt long. After that, you'll get a whole new high. Better than what you have ever experienced." Trevor pulled out a needle and mixed some stuff up. Next, he found what he thought was a good vein on Kelly's arm, stuck the needle in, and gave him the shot of drugs.

Kelly's head was turned; he felt the "prick," and it did hurt, but definitely not for long. Because Kelly was taken to a new level of high, just like Trevor said. As Kelly was floating away to bliss, he asked Trevor, "What was that stuff?"

"It's called methamphetamine. It is a type of speed.

You'll be up for a while, but enjoy the ride. You'll be back for more."

Trevor wasn't kidding when he said Kelly would be up for a while. He was up for three days, climbing the walls and grinding his teeth. After he came down off the high he realized he actually hated it. He hated being up for three days, his eyes burning because he wanted to sleep but couldn't, and the feeling of the jitters was unstoppable. *Surely there is something else out there that would help me escape to another world without making me feel like a speed freak.*

You're really going to like this. It's cocaine.

The next week at another party Kelly saw Trevor and approached him, "Hey, man, that stuff was awful. It was okay for a little while, but not worth the three days, bro. You gotta have somethin' better than that crud!"

A sly smile came on Trevor's face as he said, "I knew you would be back. Yeah, I got something. Let's find a little more private place." They both walked out of the room and found another one, where no one was. "You're really going to like this. It's cocaine. I know you've heard of it. But for guys your age it's not always easy to come by."

Trevor got out another syringe, and just as Kelly turned his head, he felt the "prick" again, and it didn't take long. *This is what I've been waiting for. This is what I wanted. This is it. This is what I want.*

Kelly found himself going to Trevor, and other connections he had found, to get the cocaine he needed for his fix. He was always chasing the last high. It helped him escape temporarily, but it was never enough. Nothing filled that void. Sure, he found enjoyment in some things. But nothing satisfied. There was a hunger inside of him that was never quenched, no matter how much coke he shot up.

*****

Time passed quickly, and soon Kelly had been selling dope for about a year. He carried and sold mostly smaller quantities. The older guys knew the cops wouldn't think a fourteen-year-old would be carrying drugs. But Kelly was carrying drugs, and he was good at hiding them. He would conceal the dope in different places in his room and only carry a small amount with him. His street smarts were keened in at a young age.

Kelly was out and about with his friend George when they stopped at the dope man's house to pick up one of Kelly's larger packages of pot. He already had some people lined up to buy it—plus he wanted some for himself. After they picked up their score, they left for Kelly's house, where it would be stashed until it was distributed.

They were on Kelly's street and just few blocks from his house when they noticed a car following them. Kelly pointed the car out to George. "Hey, man, that car looks suspicious. It just doesn't fit this neighborhood. Make sure you go the speed limit. We don't need to draw attention to us."

As soon as the words left his mouth, police cars surrounded them. There was no running. George stopped and put the car in park.

The policemen were out of their squad cars in less than a minute and yelling at the two boys to get out of the vehicle. Trying to hide their fear, George and Kelly got out of the car with "Mr. Attitude" written all over them.

The policemen knew both boys. When George started mouthing back at them, one of the police officers hit him with the butt of his pistol to shut him up.

Kelly was acting as if he was twenty instead of fourteen.

The police always saw him walking around the neighborhood and knew he was trouble, but they had never been able to catch him in anything. This time they had something to pin on him.

As Kelly was arguing with one of the police officers, he looked up toward his house and saw his mom standing outside, watching in disbelief. His stomach sank. Although he gave her problems, he never wanted her to see him being arrested. He knew getting caught might happen one day, but not like this. Not with her seeing it all. All he could see was her beehive hairdo, and her head shaking back and forth, like she was trying to tell herself it wasn't her son being arrested.

The cop put Kelly in the back seat of the undercover car and then went to talk to Virginia. "Kelly is in big trouble this time, ma'am."

Virginia was shaking and crying at the same time. "What did he do?" she asked, even though she really didn't want to know the truth.

"He had ten pounds of marijuana, and a pair of brass knuckles. We've been watching him, but never had anything solid until today. This time we saw him leave a known drug dealer's house. You see, they use younger teenagers to run their dope because the sentencing is a little more lenient on the younger ones than the older ones. He's smart, but that street smart is going to lead him down a long road to a bad place."

Virginia was numb. "What do I need to do now?" she asked, her tone subdued.

"There is nothing for you to do, Mrs. Downing. Right now we're going to take him in for questioning. You'll most likely be able to come pick him up tomorrow."

"Okay. Thank you."

As the police officer walked away, Virginia went inside. She told herself she hadn't known Kelly was dealing drugs—but then how could she lie to herself? She had seen some of the signs, but just didn't want to believe it of her son. She dreaded telling Vernon about it. But then, he would find out sooner or later. She just knew it would push him and Kelly even further away from each other.

Whatever happened to the father inside Vernon? The one who used his savings to hire a private investigator to search for Kelly when Barbara took him? That seems like ages ago. Everything is different now. Gone were the days of being a young couple, happy with a new son. Now, Vernon was bitter and miserable, and wanted everyone around him to be miserable, too. He definitely put forth a concerted effort for them to be.

Is this just the beginning of Kelly's troubles? Virginia wondered to herself.

CHAPTER
~ *Six* ~

Kelly was sentenced to Gainesville State School for twelve months. He would be able to go home on furlough after eight months, and then back again. The judge said this was one step in state prison, and one step out. If he continued down this same road, he would definitely end up in the Texas Department of Criminal Justice. The judge just hoped that sending Kelly to reform school would scare him so that he wouldn't continue dealing drugs.

The hardest part for Kelly was that Gainesville was north of Dallas, which meant it was five hours away from home. He wouldn't be able to see his mom as often as he had the last time he was sent to a juvenile center. No homemade pies this time. He was on his own.

Gainesville State School was a lot different than the Harris County Youth Village. It was jail, but for juveniles. He was locked up in a cell with no cellmate. He didn't even have much school work to do to pass the time. The kids were a little older, and some had done more serious crimes. It was going to be a long eight months.

However, Kelly soon fell into a routine again. He was

afraid of no one and let it be known by never backing down from a fight. The kids there found out real quick that Kelly wasn't just another guy they could push around. As soon as someone started in on him, Kelly was all over them. Whether it was with verbal assaults or fist fights, Kelly got his message across that you didn't want to mess with him. It only took a few scuffles for him to accomplish his goal.

He found a few guys to hang out with, but he never let his guard down and never let anyone too close emotionally. He kept his cool and had a good reputation with the staff, so that helped him get by in the system—the staff were a little more lenient with the "good" kids. Kelly learned early on when to turn on his charm and how to use it to his advantage. He was always the life of the party because he learned humor helped ease pain, and when others laughed at his jokes and humor, it made him feel good.

Going through the motions was something Kelly was good at. He would go to what limited class they had, go to meal time, go to rec time, and go to bed. The worst part was the fact that it was the same daily grind. And it was boring. And these meals made Virginia's beans and rice and gravy sound better every day.

The eight months went by very slowly, which made Kelly glad to be going home, even if it was only for a short visit. He was ready to eat some home cooking, get back on the streets, and get his hands on some good drugs. Eight months with nothing, not even pot, had been hard for him to do. Now, homeward bound. He was sure his mom would be happy to see him. He just hoped she wouldn't cry.

*****

Kelly played the role of the good kid for a little while when he got home. The attention he got was something he hadn't known he was craving. His dad was his usual self, but his mother doted on him. He even went to church with Virginia more than he had before, because it made her so happy.

Unconsciously, Kelly manipulated his parents into thinking juvy had really changed him, that it had done some good. Since he liked the attention he was getting he kept up the front. That didn't mean he wasn't back to the smoking, shooting, and dealing; he just didn't let them know what was going on. He had regained some trust and liked it. In the back of his mind he knew that he could use that trust to his advantage.

Because his behavior had been so good in Gainesville and continued once he got home, Virginia and Vernon were able to talk the judge into letting Kelly stay home. Kelly had already gotten his hands on acid, mandrex, alcohol, mushrooms, pot, and some good coke within just a month of being home. He had fallen back into dealing and getting what he needed. Kelly prided himself on being the only fifteen-year-old he knew to be able to get his hands on the drugs that he did. And he liked his reputation of having the best dope in town.

*****

The next school year started out well. All his school friends had missed him at Lee High School. He was going into his sophomore year, not that it meant anything to him, but he did like being popular and more quick-witted than his peers. If *they only knew the stuff I did*, he thought. The parties he went to with older teenagers and adults. The drugs he sold and had in his possession. Those boring kids at school would flip!

Kelly used his good looks and charismatic personality

to get where he needed to go. He was also a good judge of character. When he was dealing, he could tell if someone was going to pay up or not. Life's lessons were hard, and he learned many of them early.

Things had been going well at school—he was present more than he was absent, and while he got into some of the normal school fights, he didn't land in major trouble. But his day was coming. Alicia, one of the girls who had recently started getting high more and more often, was grating on his nerves. Kelly and Alicia were picking back and forth at each other, but she was really getting to him and making him angrier by the minute.

He finally popped off something back to one of her smart remarks and she pulled back and slapped him across his face. That was it for Kelly. When he started in on beating her up, there was no pulling him off. He totally lost it. There was no way she could defend herself.

He beat her badly—so badly that the teachers called an ambulance to take her to the hospital. After it was all said and done, Kelly barely even remembered everything that had happened. It was almost as if he had become another person for a few minutes. He deeply regretted hurting Alicia, but because of pride he didn't show much remorse on the outside. He was still focused on presenting a cool, tough-kid exterior.

Before Kelly realized what was going on, he was sitting in Principal Sanders' office. Principal Sanders was leaning back in his chair twirling a pencil between his fingers, as if he were very comfortable with the whole situation. He didn't waste any time with small talk, but got right to the point.

"I hate doing what I am about to do. Kelly, not only have you put a girl in the hospital, but you have caused nothing but trouble here at Lee High School. You skip class sometimes and never do homework. I know your grades are decent, but that doesn't mean you're participating. You just got lucky with some smarts and can pass tests more easily than other students. I'm sure you're smoking marijuana, but we just haven't been able to catch you at it yet. And the list could go on with all the complaints from your teachers."

Principal Sanders stopped talking for a moment and studied Kelly intently. He straightened in his chair and, with a serious look on his face, continued. "After talking with the staff, I've reached a decision, and we are no longer going to allow you to come back here to school any longer. You can go to Sterling High School after six months, go to reform school, or be home-schooled if you want an education. But we cannot allow you to come here any longer."

Kelly stood. "Well, then. I guess I don't need to be here anymore." With that he left the office and the school.

Kelly didn't care about being kicked out. He knew he could go to Sterling High—he would just wait six months and then enroll. Since it was still the beginning of the school year, he could finish out the last semester there.

*****

The six months had flown by for Kelly, and he was already deep into the second semester at Sterling. During the six months he had kept up his usual game, but was able to stay under the radar of his parents. Now that school was back in full swing, he wasn't sure how he liked it. He knew a lot of the kids, but it wasn't the same as being with his old friends. He ended up skipping school most of the time, and when he was there he wasn't involved at all. He didn't even try when it came to test time. His grades were down, and the teachers were not pleased with his academic performance.

Before the school year was up Kelly was called into Principal Wilson's office. Principal Wilson was not happy with Kelly's conduct in school, and let him know that from the moment Kelly entered the office. "You haven't shown any interest in your academics since you enrolled. Your teachers tell me you don't participate in anything. So let me ask you: Why are you here?"

Kelly showed no emotion and simply answered, "Because I have to be."

Principal Wilson waited a minute before replying. "If you don't want to be here, then we don't want to waste our time. You can leave any time you want. Ain't nobody making you come. If you drop out, you'll probably end up on the streets and not have any kind of life. But," he took a deep breath and then let it out, "that's your choice."

Kelly stood and said, "Well, if it's my choice, then I'm gone. None of y'all care anyway. If you don't care, then why should I care?" He stormed out, slamming the door behind him.

Vernon was already home when Kelly walked in the door. "What are you doing home?" he asked in a level voice, but he knew something was up, because Kelly was home much earlier than normal. Vernon's anger was already starting to boil.

Kelly stood tall and with pride in his voice said, "I quit school. I am not going back. The school doesn't care, Principal Wilson doesn't care, and so I don't care."

Vernon had been furious when Kelly had been expelled from Lee High School. But being kicked out a second time! Vernon was beyond angry. It took a moment for him to respond, but when he did, he let Kelly know just how low he thought he was. The venomous words spewed from his mouth, each one coated with anger and character assassination. He ended with,

"I should have known you were going to be a good for nothin'."

There was only one thing for Kelly to do, and it was something he had practiced and learned well through the years. He would harden his heart against his father's words, pretend they didn't bother him, get high, and go where he had earned his respect: the streets of Baytown. Through gritted teeth he forced the words, "What you say doesn't mean anything because you don't mean anything. You're not my dad and never will be." With that Kelly walked into his bedroom, grabbed his stash, and was out the door.

CHAPTER
~ *Seven* ~

Three years of dealing had earned Kelly quite a reputation, both on the streets and in the police station. The cops were always watching him, but he was slick and cautious—they couldn't find anything to charge him with. Even though he was young, his word had influence on the streets, and the police knew it. He thrived on the power he had worked hard to gain. If he wanted someone brought down, he could get it done. If he wanted cocaine, he could get it. If he wanted the ladies, he could get them.

Virginia and Vernon didn't like how Kelly earned his money, and neither did the rest of their family. Eventually, all of his family but his adoptive parents became emotionally distant and refused to be around him. Although his family members may have had their reasons, their distance only proved to harden Kelly's heart and push him away even more. The only place he felt at home was on the streets, but he never trusted anyone. He had learned early on to never let his guard down, because there was always someone waiting to stab him in the back.

By the time Kelly was seventeen, he was bringing in good money through dealing drugs. He had left home and was living with friends, and even had a new girlfriend, Jeane. He liked her, but he still didn't let anyone too close to him. He knew things were bad at home for Jeane, but didn't realize how bad until she approached him one day.

"Kelly, I don't know what I'm going to do anymore. I just don't think I can live at home much longer. My dad is doing things with my friends that he shouldn't be doing. I can't stay there. And when I want to escape from reality, the drugs only last for a little while, and they only numb the pain. They don't change things."

They talked for a while about different scenarios, until Kelly finally said, "Look, there's nowhere really for you to go. I'm working now, and bringing in decent money. Why don't you move in with me and the guys? There isn't much more of an option. That seems to be the best thing to do."

She hesitated for a minute before saying, "Okay. I think I could do that." She thought a few more minutes. "Yeah, that would be good. Thanks, Kelly."

After several months of living together they decided to get married. It wasn't the romantic type of marriage Jeane would have liked, but she dealt with it—at least it had gotten her out of her father's house, though at one point when they had nowhere else to go they were forced to move to San Antonio and stay with him for a short time. They smoked pot together and Kelly continued to abuse cocaine. He worked long, hard hours. After their honeymoon phase faded, Jeane learned all about Kelly's quick temper. In fact, she got the brunt of it most of the time.

Life was becoming unbearable, especially because in only a year Kelly's drug use had become much worse. He would stay gone for days at a time, or just lock himself in a room to shoot up. After the high and the money were gone, Kelly's temper always got the best of him. Sometimes he would work and sometimes he wouldn't. Jeane was growing more tired of him, and she didn't like being afraid of her own husband. While she liked marijuana, she couldn't tolerate the cocaine use. She wouldn't have to deal with it much longer, though, because Kelly's mistakes would soon catch up with him.

Before they had gotten married, Kelly had been arrested and was charged with possession of a controlled substance. He had known this day might come, but he didn't expect to get so lucky with the judge's sentence. Instead of time in prison, he

The police sent him to jail, where he was sentenced to two years...

received deferred adjudication with only two years' probation. However, his luck didn't hold. Kelly's arrest had made him more cautious—but he never stopped dealing or shooting up. On his third probation office visit, he failed the urinalysis. The police sent him to jail, where he was sentenced to two years in the Texas Department of Criminal Justice.

When he was on the Jester Unit, Jeane came to visit him. "I am nervous about us and about what's going to happen. What am I going to do while you're gone for two years? Since I didn't have anywhere to live, I had to move back in with my dad. I don't know how much longer I can do this."

Kelly tried to reassure her and tell her the time would go by quickly. He knew she wasn't buying it, but he tried to convince himself otherwise. The visit was too short, and there wasn't enough time to discuss everything that needed to be discussed.

The next day Kelly was served with divorce papers. He was floored, but showed no emotion. As he lay in bed that night his mind was on the notice he received. Jeane was divorcing him, and there was nothing he could do about it because he was in jail.

1984 Booking Picture

I knew she was different yesterday. I knew she was up to something. I just never expected her to do this. Now I have two years to face in jail alone, with no one. I am going to get straightened out. I am going to get clean while I am in here. I still have my whole life ahead of me. If I straighten up now I can make something of myself. I have to do this.

Any thought of God had been abandoned a long time ago, so there was no "leaning on the everlasting arm" for Kelly. He never once thought about turning to God to deal with the pain and addiction. In his mind, he only had himself. There was no one else.

*****

The first time down was harder than Kelly could've ever imagined. There was no adjusting, because it wasn't something he wanted to adjust to. There were fights every day, as well as gang activity; each ethnicity was against the other. He tried to stay out of all the cliques and keep to himself, and with no group behind him to protect him he got jumped a few times and beaten up badly. But he put up a good fight. The men soon learned that this young, skinny kid would fight to the end. He could give some punches and take some, too.

It didn't take long for Kelly to learn the ropes. There were some inmates who were trustees, called "building tenders." Anyone who had to go to the doctor or take care of other matters had to go to them. If the building tenders liked you, you could go. If they didn't, you were stuck out. This system didn't seem fair, but there wasn't anything Kelly could do about it.

The hardest time seemed to be recreation time, when everyone got together in one large area. Other than during chow time, rec time was when most of the fights happened. And today was one of those days. There had been a few fights already, and tension was thick in the air. One older man turned to Kelly and said, "Boy, you betta watch yo back and everyone around you. There's a riot 'bout to break out. You best be thinking of a weapon other than yo fists, 'cause they ain't gonna get you very far."

Kelly looked at him fearlessly and replied, "I'm watching. I'm even watching you, because I don't trust nobody."

"You got spunk kid. Jus' don't get all arrogant. You might jus' make it."

A minute later the riot broke out, all races against each other. Kelly felt like he was fighting a war. He was dodging punches, throwing punches, fighting for his very life. He barely missed being shanked by a toothbrush that had been filed down to make a weapon, and after trying to get out of the middle of the fray he found himself up against the fence with nowhere else to go. When he saw someone coming for him he turned and started climbing the fence, kicking anyone who was under him.

The next thing he heard was gun shots going off. He dropped to the ground from the fence and the riot started breaking up. The guards came out with the dogs and went for some of the men they suspected of starting it. Everyone else was made to go back to their cells.

When Kelly woke up the next morning, his body was sore and aching. He had a busted nose, a black eye, and bruises all over, but luckily no broken bones. The riot wasn't something he wanted to go through again, but somehow he knew he would. That afternoon he found out from another inmate that he was on one of the worst prison units. They had had life flight helicopters there 370 times in one year because of the fighting and riots. Wow, what a way to get broke in good, he thought to himself.

*****

In prison you didn't stay at one farm too long before you got moved again and every farm was different. Different atmospheres, different mindsets, different regulations. The warden ran things, and he made the rules.

The months went by slowly, but though Kelly would be getting out soon, any time spent in prison was too long. There were no phone calls and no letters. He had to get by with only what the prison offered, and it was the cheapest of necessities, such as powder for toothpaste. He didn't have the luxury of going and buying name brand items at commissary, so he did what he had to just to get by. He couldn't wait to get out and go home.

CHAPTER
~ *Eight* ~

Kelly wasn't exactly sure what to expect when he got out, but he hoped things were better. It was already bad enough that he had gone in to prison married and had come out divorced. He just wanted to see his family. While he and the Downings may have had their differences, they were the only family he had, and he missed them.

After Kelly was released, he got what he never expected: positive attention from everyone. Of course, it wasn't like they were used to family members going to prison, but they were sure that prison had helped change him and broken his addiction to drugs. He was in good spirits, and everyone was so happy to see him. He was even able to take it easy for a little while at home, enjoying his freedom, before anyone said anything about him going to work.

While Virginia felt bad about not having written many letters to Kelly, she had prayed constantly for her son; he had always been in her thoughts. She knew God's hand was on Kelly's life, even though it hadn't appeared to be so at the time he was arrested. His heart had seemed to callous over, but she never gave up hope. She tried to think on the positive, even though oftentimes the negative came out.

Since Kelly had gotten out of prison, her hopes were higher than before. Kelly's attitude was better, his thinking was clearer, and he was more courteous. This was the son she knew she had, not the hardened criminal and dopehead others painted him out to be. Only a mother could look past the hardness into the soul of her son and see the person who God truly wanted him to be. It was this mother's love that she tried to show Kelly.

When she got home from work one afternoon, Virginia found that Vernon and Kelly had fixed dinner. She thought that was nice of them, and was also happy that they were getting along well enough to do something together without harsh words or bitterness. She knew she would still have to clean up, but at least she had come home to a meal already prepared. The two men were watching Monday Night Football and the Raiders were on, one of Vernon's favorite teams. Since Kelly was in one of the best moods he'd been in for a long time, Virginia ventured a bold question during the commercial break. "Kelly, what do think about going to church with me Sunday? I'm sure everyone would love to see you—they've all been praying for you." She waited hopefully as she watched the hesitancy move across his face.

"Yeah, I think I could go." He paused and then continued, "I hope they're not expecting much from me, because I'm only going for you, and for nothing else."

Virginia couldn't ask for anything more. "Thank you, son. That means a lot to me." She stopped talking when the game came back on, because she knew his attention would be averted to it rather than on church. She also knew she couldn't push him. The fact that he had decided to come was huge all in itself. Perhaps once he came to church, God would lead him back into the fold.

When Sunday morning came, Kelly kept true to his word. He asked Virginia, "What time do we need to be ready to leave by?"

"Around 9:45."

"Okay, you're always running late to everything. You'll be late for your own funeral, for Pete's sake. You say 9:45, so that means we will leave by 10:15," he said sarcastically.

"Oh hush!" she said emphatically. "I'll be ready on time."

Kelly looked at her doubtfully before walking away to finish getting dressed.

They were gone by 10:00. At least they would only be a little late.

Kelly barely paid attention to the preaching, because he didn't believe anything anyway. He had convinced himself early on that none of this was real. People weren't supposed to worship loudly, and they didn't really speak in tongues "as the Spirit gave utterance." But while he may not have believed anything, he still tried to be cordial, because it was important to Virginia.

After the service, Kelly was surprised that he received a warm welcome from everyone. They greeted him with hugs. Many of them remembered him as a little boy and said they had been praying for him. Some of the older women even pinched him on the cheek. However, since he hadn't eaten breakfast, his mind was more on the roast in the oven at home than on catching up with the congregation. He was glad when he and his mother had greeted the last people and made their way home. Virginia made small talk about some of the people and what they had been going through lately, and how God had carried them through their times of trial. He half listened and half didn't.

After being out for a little over a month now, his mind was going back to his old friends and connections. Part of him was missing the life he had made for himself over two years ago. Although no one had written him, he knew they were probably still working the streets—you didn't just get out of this lifestyle overnight, unless you were arrested or killed.

*****

It had only been four months since Kelly was released from prison. So far he had been able to stay clean and was attending the Narcotics Anonymous classes required by the court as part of his parole and rehabilitation. He had even started back to work as a roofer. It was hard, physical labor, but he was good at it and confident in what he was doing. He could tear off a whole roof by himself in one day and lay it all the next day, depending on the size of the roof. The homeowners liked him because he was polite and had a great personality, and this helped him find favor in the boss's eyes.

However, he realized that he couldn't fight the cravings to do the drugs again. He went through the motions of making the phone call, to setting up the sell, to how he would leave, to where he would go, to the feel of the prick of the needle, and to the expected high itself. Those fantasies haunted him all throughout the day and night, and he knew it was only a matter of time before he gave in.

Once he started back to the drugs, he told himself he could control it to just occasional use. That he didn't really need it often. He didn't even need to sell it. He could just do it while at parties or while he was chilling by himself. He continued to lie to himself about how in control he was.

After several months Virginia began to see some of

Kelly's angry attitudes come back. She knew he had fallen back into the old routine. Even the rest of the family could see the difference in him. She was greatly discouraged, because she had thought for sure he was over the addiction. With two years clean, how could he possibly

No one had ever taught her how to confront someone addicted to cocaine.

go back to it? She didn't know how to deal with him, or even how to talk to him about it. No one had ever taught her how to confront someone addicted to cocaine. She acted the only way she knew how, and that was to pretend like nothing was wrong.

*****

The months slipped by, and Kelly's condition continued to deteriorate. Virginia had just finished dinner one night when Kelly walked in. This last year he had been in and out a lot, sometimes staying with her and Vernon and sometimes staying at friends' houses. Nothing was consistent in his life. She never knew what to expect or what kind of phone call she was going to get. At least he looked decent and clean today.

"What's for dinner, Mom?"

"Pork chops and rice with mashed potatoes and pinto beans." She thought back over the last month to the recent events. Kelly had been a passenger during a car wreck and was supposed to settle with the insurance company any time now for his part of the claim. She knew he was supposed to talk to the insurance company today. "What did the insurance company tell you today when you talked to them?"

While filling his plate, he replied, "They said after the hospital costs and all I should get about $10,000. I am happy with that. It will be enough to buy a dependable truck. Once I get the money and the truck, I'll also need to get my license. I'm twenty years old, so I think it's about time I get my driver's license." He smiled real big at Virginia, then went and sat down to eat.

Virginia fixed her plate and then joined him. She knew Vernon would be home any minute now, too, but Kelly would probably already have eaten and be gone by the time he got home. That was fine with Virginia—they didn't get along at all, and it wore her out trying to play peacemaker.

*****

Kelly finally got the insurance money and bought the truck he had had his eye on. He was on his way to the DMV, excited to finally get his license. He waited in line for what seemed like forever until the teller looked at him and said, "Next in line."

When he walked up to her window he said, "I need to see about getting my driver's license."

"How old are you?"

Kelly tried not to get impatient when he answered, "I'm twenty years old, ma'am."

She handed him a clipboard and said, "I'm going to need you to fill out this paperwork, and I'll need to see your birth certificate."

Her asking for his birth certificate caught him off guard. "My birth certificate? I was adopted. I've never even seen my birth certificate, ma'am. What do you expect me to do?"

She looked at him with a cocky attitude. "Well, I guess you're not going to get a driver's license until you find you a birth certificate saying you're an American citizen and of the right age."

Kelly slammed the clipboard on the counter and stormed out.

He was waiting for Virginia when she got home. He told her about what happened at the DMV and asked her about his birth certificate.

She was anxious about answering him. She had thought she could avoid this, but she was wrong. She knew Kelly's temper was going to flare. "I have your birth certificate. Hold on just a minute and let me go find it."

He saw the nervousness on her face and knew there was something else. He was growing more impatient and wanted to know what was going on. By the time Virginia got back with the birth certificate his patience had already worn thin.

"Here you go. You see, we got legal custody of you, but your name was never legally changed

The name "Samuel Douglas Caywood" stare back at him.

from the name you were born with to the name we gave you. Your legal name is Samuel Douglas Caywood."

He stared down at the birth certificate in total shock. He hadn't been expecting this. The name "Samuel Douglas Caywood" stared back at him. It took him a few minutes to respond. "Do you mean that y'all took me in, and so-called adopted me, but you didn't even care enough about me to give me your name? To make me a Downing instead of this Caywood fellow? I don't even know who this is. And this is supposed to be my name. This is who I am supposed to go by?" He was yelling by now. Hurt, anger, pain, shock, and confusion were just a few of the emotions he was feeling. "I can't believe y'all would do that! I see just how much you consider me to be your son."

He took his birth certificate and left for the dope house. That was the only thing he knew would numb the pain. As if finding out at eleven years old that he was adopted wasn't hard enough, he had just realized that the name he had grown up with all of his life wasn't even his legal name. This only reinforced the identity crisis in his life. Now he didn't even know who he was. This set him on a whole new level of searching for himself, and he ended up back on the streets, where at least everyone knew who he was.

CHAPTER
~ *Nine* ~

Kelly was still getting high, but was having a harder time getting money since he hadn't had a steady job in the last month. He was out walking around and had just done his last shot of dope an hour earlier whenever he started craving another. He knew his suppliers wouldn't front him anymore because he already owed them money. He started getting desperate and thinking irrational thoughts.

Still high, he grabbed a ratchet and rag. He threw the rag over a ratchet, trying to make it look like a gun. He walked into a Jack In The Box fast-food restaurant and proceeded to rob the cashier. When everyone ran to the back screaming, he tried to open the cash register. When the cash register wouldn't open he tried to take it off the counter. Finding that it was bolted down and that he wasn't going to be able to get any money, he ran out of the restaurant.

He had never had a problem with the police when he had robbed before, but then, he had only robbed his family before. Family doesn't call the police, but restaurants do.

The police caught up with him a few blocks down. At the

Baytown City Jail, the deputies were having way too much fun on his behalf. "You're going down this time, Downing. Oh yeah, you now have an 'aka,' Mr. Caywood. I know you've been in for some misdemeanor arrests here and there over the last couple of years. But this time we got you with attempted robbery. That's a felony offense." Deputy Carlton laughed aloud. "It's men like you that keep me in my job. We don't like you no good dope dealers any way." He continued on his tirade, but Kelly had already tuned him out.

All of the Baytown police liked messing with him about his name. They couldn't just say, "Kelly Downing." They would say real sarcastically, "Stephen Kelly Downing aka Samuel Douglas Caywood," with an overemphasis on the "aka." Since he had gotten his driver's license and been in and out of the Baytown City Jail over the last couple of years for some misdemeanors, they had come to know him pretty well.

He knew he was going to go back to prison again, but now it was time for the waiting game. He had gone through this process before. Sit at the Baytown City Jail, then go to the Harris County Jail in downtown Houston to wait for his court date and sentencing.

*****

The Goree Unit in Huntsville wasn't anything nice; it was a barebones processing prison farm. Everyone who got sentenced had to come here for what the authorities called "diagnostics." The inmates got all their hair cut off, received prison uniforms, and went through a medical evaluation before going on to their assigned farm.

Kelly felt like the state was treating them like livestock, herding them through the system and prodding them when necessary. You came to the Goree Unit to be processed into TDCJ, and you went to the Walls Unit in Huntsville on your way out of the system. The system had a sick way of reminding you where you were, because for anyone to leave the Walls Unit they had to pass by the lethal injection chambers.

Kelly felt like an animal going through the processing plant. His life slowly being drained from him. But who could he blame? It was his own actions that had landed him here. The judge sentenced him to four years with a chance at parole. Kelly wondered how many prison farms he would go to this time, and if the time would go by just as slowly as it had the last time he was behind bars.

The next eight months dragged just as slowly as he

1987 Booking Picture

remembered. He wrote to the parole board for early release and parole, telling them about how he had attended classes for drug rehabilitation and was even going to be getting his GED from the Wyndham School District.

Kelly found out that TDCJ had done away with the building tenders since last time, which was a good thing in his opinion, but the fighting was still just as bad. It didn't matter what farm you were on—there were going to be fights. They may have had *different* atmospheres, but they were all *bad* atmospheres. The men inside were criminals, and angry, and looking for ways to release their rage. Kelly couldn't wait to get out.

*****

By the time the parole board had allowed Kelly to go home on parole, he had served fourteen months. He had received a few letters, but no visits and no phone calls. He had even managed to add a few more prison farms he had been to under his belt.

Now, he was on his way to the Walls Unit to be released. He would catch a bus to downtown Houston so he could meet up with his family. Kelly promised himself that he would never again go back to prison. He wanted to try and stay away from the drugs as much as possible, and not get caught doing anything illegal to put him back in the slammer. His mind was made up: he would try and be a new man.

Everyone seemed so happy to see him again, much like they had last time. Vernon was even somewhat glad to welcome him home. This surprised Kelly, since Vernon had never seemed to care one way or another. Everyone made excuses as to why they didn't write, saying that life was just too busy. Of course, who was Kelly to cast blame on them—it had been his own actions that had resulted in his arrest. But the lack of letters did make him feel unloved and unwanted.

It didn't take long to get back in to the swing of things. Kelly was able to find a job soon after he got out. He was even able to borrow the truck sometimes when Vernon didn't need it.

Kelly knew something was wrong with his mom, but he couldn't figure out what it was. It was normal for her to come home and read in the evenings instead of facing some of life's situations. Kelly knew the façade she put up very well, because she had acted similarly many times in the past when he had hit rock bottom with the drugs. When he couldn't take her distance and silence anymore, he sought her out and found her on the front porch reading.

He sat down beside her. "So what's been bothering you, Mom?"

She set her book on her lap and just looked at him. He knew she was either trying to figure out how to get out of telling him, or trying to figure out how to tell him. He spoke in the most comforting and gentle tone possible. "Just tell me what it is. Tell me straight out."

After a moment Virginia finally found her voice. "While you were in jail we found out some bad news about your dad." She paused. Kelly was patient and was going to let her take as long as she needed to in telling him what was wrong. "He had been feeling weak for a little while, but just dismissed it. While he was on the jobsite out at the Arco plant he fell down, just all of a sudden. He didn't have hardly any strength in his legs. Since it gave everyone a scare, they made him go to the hospital."

She stopped for a minute again as if in deep thought, then let out a long sigh and said, "After a few tests, they diagnosed him with multiple sclerosis."

Kelly wasn't sure what to think. "What is multiple sclerosis?"

"It's an autoimmune disease where your body attacks the myelin sheath, a protective covering, around your nerves. When the myelin sheath is torn down from around your nerves, you have what is similar to a short circuit in electricity when the wire is bare without the conduit. The nerve impulse from your brain never gets all the way to the muscle. The weakness he was feeling was because his brain was sending signals to his muscles to move, but not all of the signals got there, and so his muscles didn't move."

"So, what does this mean? How does it affect his life? Can he work? Will he die from it?" While there were times he really didn't like Vernon, Vernon was still his dad, and Kelly did love him. Even though Kelly despised him, he still loved him.

"He can work for now sometimes. He's in the beginning stages, where the weakness and symptoms come and go for periods of time. He can work a while, and then he will have to quit or get laid off and draw unemployment. Eventually he will not be able to work and will have to draw social security. He will still live for a long time, but he can die from it. There will come a time when his organs won't receive the signals from his brain to function properly, and they will shut down, and he will die." She took a deep breath and let it out. "This has just all been very hard to deal with. We will end up having to take care of him in the end. Right now it's not that bad, but one day it will be. And that thought is just hard to deal with."

Kelly felt the weight of the situation and knew things were going to be hard on her. He told himself that he wanted to be there for her when the need arose. He wanted to try and lighten the burden of having to care for his dad. He wondered what effect this was having on Vernon. By the way Vernon acted, it had no effect at all. He would probably always be sarcastic and ornery.

Virginia and Kelly sat outside and talked for quite a while. Whenever they came inside Virginia let Vernon know that she had told Kelly about the multiple sclerosis. Vernon looked at Kelly and said sarcastically, "Yeah, I'm sick. But I'll make it. What are you going to do now that you know? Are you going to run to Mother Cocaine? She'll take care of you, she always does."

All the sentiments Kelly had toward Vernon about the situation left, and in their place stood anger toward him. "Why can't you talk about the situation without bringing up drugs? Just as I am going to the court-ordered drug classes and trying to get past the addictions you want to throw it back in my face!"

It was only a minute before Kelly's voice was raised in anger. But the anger was really only a front to mask the hurt Vernon had just inflicted. "You sound like that's what you expect from me. Like the only thing I am capable of doing is drugs. I don't think you ever believed in me. If you did, you sure have a messed up way of showing it. Oh, I could bring up the past and all of your failures, too. Do you want me to do that? No, you don't. I know I've done my share of wrong. I know I've stolen things. I know the pain I've caused Mom. Don't you think I know what I have done! I don't need you reminding me of them."

Kelly walked into his room and then to the front door. He looked at Virginia sitting on the couch, not knowing what to do. Ignoring Vernon he said, "I am going out for a little while. Don't wait up for me, because I don't know when I'll be back."

Vernon shot Kelly a nasty look and asked, "Where are you going?"

Kelly knew what kind of answer he wanted, but he wasn't going to give him the satisfaction of it. "Just away from you." With that he left the house and went for a short walk to blow off some steam before going to a friend's house not far away.

*****

As the months went by Kelly's drug use became more apparent again. He found himself at some very low points and was often without food and shelter. He showed up at home one night when it was cold outside. He was high, out of money, and shivering. The door was locked, so he had to knock, and when his mom came to the door, he saw the pain in her eyes. He asked her if he could come in, but he wasn't sure how she would answer. She had let him in many times in the past, but she knew when he was getting high it was only a matter of time before he stole something and was out the door not many hours later. This time she never let him past the door—she just dropped her head and cried. "You look like death warmed over, Kelly. I can't stand to see you like this. Please don't come here high again. I can't take it." Then she shut the door.

How could he blame her? He couldn't bear to look at himself, either. He was way too skinny, his eyes were almost protruding out of his face, and he hadn't showered in days. He felt so bound by the drugs that he couldn't help but believe that he was destined to do them for the rest of his life. No matter how hard he tried, he never could get past the addiction. The only way he knew to cope with life was with the drugs, and so he kept turning to them to deal with his pain.

> *You look like death warmed over, Kelly. I can't stand to see you like this.*

*****

A few days later, after Kelly had ran out of money and cleaned up some, he was able to come home for a few days. Vernon had grown tired of Kelly's ups and downs, and while he didn't know what to do with him, he had reached the end of his rope. Vernon told Kelly he wanted to go for a ride, and Kelly agreed, though wary of Vernon's friendliness toward him. They stopped at the store, where they got a pack of cigarettes, then headed to old Baytown.

Kelly couldn't figure out where they were going. Vernon had a few friends in this part of town, but not many. This was where he had always scored dope, but he didn't know why his dad would need to come to this part of town. "Why are we over here?"

Vernon had stayed quiet most of the time. He had had enough of Kelly, and was about to show him. "If all you want is the drugs, then I'm going to help you. I am sick of your lifestyle. You're not even trying to stay sober, so why don't you just stay high. At least you stay away when you're high."

Kelly looked at him in astonishment. He couldn't believe what he had just heard, and he certainly didn't know how to reply to it. Vernon pulled over just down the road from the dope house, reached into his pocket, and pulled out twenty dollars. He said, "If drugs are what you want, then you can have them. Here's twenty dollars. I hope this is the shot that kills you. Now get out."

All Kelly could do was drop his head and get out of the truck. Never in his life had he expected to hear such words from his dad. Sure, Vernon had said some hurtful things in the past, but he had never even come close to saying that he wished Kelly would die. *How could things have ever gotten to this point?* He was sure his dad was secretly scared about his diagnosis, and Kelly knew he had done some bad things toward him, but he still couldn't believe his dad would say such things.

With his thoughts filled with pain and confusion, Kelly did what his dad told him. He went and got some cocaine and did the only thing he knew to do.

*****

Work wasn't ever hard to come by for Kelly, because he had always been a hard worker. Whether it was roofing, building construction, pipe fitting, welding, or boiler making, he always managed to keep a job for at least long enough to get on his feet.

When Kelly was on his bad drug binges he tried not to go around Virginia much, because he knew it would only hurt her. With nowhere to stay he rented a cheap motel room. Most of his money was going to drugs, and he sometimes didn't even have enough for food. When there was almost no money he managed to at least get some bread, even though it wasn't much.

He was now working as a boiler maker and doing a lot of work in tall towers. How he kept his job was beyond him. He almost always had cocaine on him when he went to work and would do a shot at some point during the day. He was putting himself and others in danger, but he didn't care.

He found himself always chasing that next high, but it was never enough. He was miserable, and nothing filled the void inside. The dope only masked it and made him feel numb to it all for a little while. His insecurities and self-esteem were at an all-time low. He felt like a failure in everything he did.

After Kelly got paid Friday night, he bought some lunch meat and bread, went to the dope house, and then returned to the motel. He had already been getting high, but he was tired of the high without the satisfaction.

I don't know what I am even doing here. I don't deserve

to live. There's nothing in life for me. I can't achieve anything. I am a failure at everything. I don't have anything to show for my life except for scars and pain. My family doesn't want me. The best thing I can do for me and everyone else is to just end my life. Maybe I should get a gun? No, that would be too brutal.

He looked at the cocaine he had left. It was enough to do several more shots through the night and into tomorrow. *I could put all of that dope into a syringe and shoot it all up. That would be more than enough to make me overdose and kill myself. I've seen people OD on less than half of that.*

I could put all of that dope into a syringe and shoot it all up. That would be more than enough to make me overdose and kill myself.

He mixed it with some water, drew it all up into a syringe, and shot it up. Within a few minutes he found himself slipping into utter darkness, sure he was on his way to death.

The next day Kelly came to in his motel room. After realizing he had not died, but had only blacked out, he screamed, "Jesus! I can't even die right! Why? Why can't I just die? I don't want to live! I just want to die!" He was sick more so than ever before, but he was sicker at the fact that he hadn't died.

CHAPTER
~ Ten ~

A few months had gone by since the suicide attempt in the motel; afterwards, Kelly just went on with life. Though he had recently gotten fired from work after someone reported him for carrying drugs, he managed to find occasional odd jobs and survive.

Since he was between steady jobs, Kelly took some time off to visit friends in the nearby city of Channelview for a few days. Kelly had managed to say clean for a few weeks, but the city was known for being a bad area, with drugs running rampant. Tonight he and his friends were watching a game, smoking marijuana, and drinking. Kelly had always said he didn't have a drinking problem, and that his addiction was drugs. But recently he realized that every time he started drinking he also wanted to get high. The same thing was happening now. He was fighting the urge just as he had before. He knew he wasn't going to be able to fight it off tonight, though. It was only a matter of time, and drugs were easy to come by in this town.

He turned to Jason. "Hey, buddy, I hope you don't mind, but I'm gonna have to call it short tonight. I need to go take care of some things."

Jason shrugged and barely took his eyes off the TV as he said, "Nah, man. I don't care. Go do what you need to do. I'll see you later."

"Thanks, bro. Check ya later." With that Kelly left the house. He went to the nearest gas station to call a cab from the pay phone. The cab showed up within five minutes, and Kelly told him the address of the dope house he knew to be close.

Kelly, naturally friendly, learned the cab driver's name to be Todd. While on the way he and Todd made small talk, and Kelly didn't think anything of it. Their conversation consisted of just basic questions: Where are you from? How old are you? What people do we both know? Kelly volunteered more information than necessary because he had been drinking—alcohol made him talkative. He even told the cabdriver that his dad had been a police officer in Baytown for a while.

Todd asked, "Oh, really?" Since they had known a few of the same people, Todd ventured, "Who is your dad?"

"Ah, you probably don't know him. He hasn't worked there in a long time."

"Try me. I was born and raised in Baytown. I just might know him."

"His name is Vernon Downing. He hasn't been on the force in while, though," Kelly warned.

Todd was silent for a minute, and he then pulled the cab over. Kelly was startled—he knew they hadn't yet reached where they was going. He raised his voice to Todd, yelling, "Hey, man, what are you doing? Why did you pull over? We aren't there yet. If my dad arrested you and you're mad, then you have to take that up with him. Bro, that ain't my fault."

Todd dropped his nonchalant, playful attitude and became very serious. "What's your real name, son?"

Kelly copped an attitude and became defensive. "Why

do you want to know?"

"Because I think I might be your uncle."

Kelly thought for a minute. "How can you be my uncle? You don't even know me."

"Were you adopted?"

"Yeah. What's that got to do with anything?"

"My sister gave up a son who would be your age, twenty-five, to a Downing family." He paused as the thought sank in for Kelly. "So what's your name?"

Kelly hesitantly said, "My adopted name is Stephen Kelly Downing, but my legal name is Samuel Douglas Caywood."

> *My sister's name is Barbara. Her son's name that she gave up was Samuel Caywood. You are my nephew.*

"My sister's name is Barbara. Her son's name that she gave up was Samuel Caywood. You are my nephew."

There were a few minutes of silence as the new knowledge sank in. Kelly had never thought he would come to know his biological mother. But here sat his biological uncle, and he probably knew where Barbara was. The information was a little overwhelming. Kelly wasn't even sure if he wanted to meet her. But he would always wonder what she was like unless he did. He asked Todd, "Do you know where she is?"

"Yes, I do. Do you want me to take you to her?"

Kelly nervously replied, "Yeah, I think I do."

"Okay. But let me call her first and make sure she's home and let her know we're coming."

After Todd stopped and made the phone call, he filled Kelly in on how Barbara was and what she was doing. Kelly learned that his biological mother lived there in Channelview, was an alcoholic, and could become violent when she started drinking. She lived an almost care-free lifestyle and didn't think much of consequences. Kelly knew that with that lifestyle she must not have much money, because it was an expensive one to live.

Kelly was extremely nervous. After they got to the house, the meeting was very emotional. Barbara had already been drinking, which made things a little awkward, though Kelly had sobered up quite a bit. All she could do was stare at him, like he had walked up out of a dream. Finally she said, "I can't believe it's you. It's really you."

He was excited about seeing her. He had questions about the past, but thought he should ask them later when they got a little more acquainted. He realized that every child who was adopted probably wanted to know who their biological parents were. Even though he still didn't know his father, he had at least been able to meet his mother. He also learned he had a few sisters. Finding out that he had a whole new family was more than a little overwhelming.

They stayed up most of the night talking and getting to know one another. He didn't go into his drug problem, but did let her know he didn't have a job at the moment and was staying with various friends. She offered him a place to stay.

Even though he wasn't working, he still had some money. Not knowing what her situation was, he offered her the money if she needed it. She laughed at him and said, "We own the only four bonded warehouses in Galveston. I have money. I thought you found me because you needed money."

This disappointed Kelly, but he didn't want to ruin a relationship that had just started. "Oh, well, I didn't know you had money. No, I don't need anything. Just a place to stay would be nice."

The next day Kelly met his youngest sister, Victoria.

She was only ten and seemed very lonely. He spent time with her, playing dolls and games. When Kelly had a chance to talk to Barbara, he asked her about the past. She had a different version of the story of Kelly's childhood, which only helped to confuse Kelly more. She said she had never wanted to give him up, but things were hard, and he wouldn't understand. Since he kept coming to dead ends with questions about the past, he decided to drop it. He was with her now, and was trying to have a relationship with her—that's what counted.

A week had gone by before Kelly realized just how bad of an alcoholic Barbara was. She was good during the day, and very nice and caring. But come afternoon time, she started drinking and became violent and hard to be around. Kelly didn't mind too much, because he got to drink, too. There always seemed to be a party going on, and Barbara had every alcoholic beverage you could think of. The sad part was that Victoria was made to stay in her room in the evenings and kept away from the adults.

Barbara eventually learned about Kelly's drug addiction, but it didn't seem to bother her any, as long as he didn't steal from her to support his habit. She was more than willing to give him money for whatever else he needed. She bought him clothes and gave him a credit card with a high balance so he could make purchases or get cash. Kelly felt like he was set. He had a roof over his head and a money supply, could get high whenever he wanted, and was getting to see his biological mother.

He told Virginia about meeting Barbara and how he was now living with her. She seemed a little disappointed at first, but said she was glad he was finally getting to know his birth mother. She voiced her concerns about him getting hurt and told him to just be careful.

It didn't take long before the daily drinking and nightly

parties and sometimes fights got old. Barbara could be downright mean and ruthless when she was drunk, and Kelly was beginning to wonder if living there was the best decision after all. He liked the free flow of cash, but after a while he really started to feel worthless. He had no life and no job, and he didn't like it at all. He was trying to figure out whether or not to stay when Barbara helped him make up his mind.

After a particularly wild party, he was fed up and had called it an early night and gone to bed. Later that night, Barbara walked in his room wearing a very thin, almost see-through night gown. She woke him up and attempted to make passes at him and flirt with him. He knew she did stupid stuff when she was drunk, but never had he expected this: His own mother being overly flirtatious with him. He made her leave the room.

The next day Kelly got his stuff together and told Barbara he had to leave. Barbara didn't even remember what happened the night before. It was probably a good thing, because it saved her some embarrassment. He figured it would be a long time before he saw her again, and that didn't sadden him any. Meeting his birth mother had not turned out like he thought it would.

CHAPTER
~ *Eleven* ~

K elly's life was spiraling downward. Just as soon as he found a job, he lost it. It had been a little harder to get back on his own again once he left Barbara's. He was able to go back home to the Downings, so at least he had a roof over his head and food to eat. Virginia didn't ask many questions about the time he had spent with Barbara, and he was glad for it. He really didn't want to talk about his birth mother or his past. He had succumbed to the truth of never having all of the answers or getting himself figured out, so he stopped trying.

Virginia and Vernon didn't know what to do with Kelly. They blamed him, then each other, then other people, until they ran out of excuses and decided that Kelly didn't truly want to quit doing drugs. Virginia would absolutely hate it whenever he would bring money for her to hold, saying he didn't want to use it to buy drugs, because he would always come back later that night, high, and demand it back.

She had seen him lose his temper before, but he had never lost it with her. She never could figure out why she would sometimes say "no" to him staying at home, and why other times she would say "yes," but more often than not she would regret letting him stay home. One time she was getting ready for work while he was watching TV, and when she came out of the bathroom he was gone, along with the TV and VCR. Incidents like that happened often, and Virginia would be so mad and hurt she would cry for hours, while Vernon ranted and raved about how bad Kelly was.

Kelly had been staying in various places when they let him come home again—Virginia knew she shouldn't, but she couldn't stand for him to be without a regular place to stay. After a little while Virginia noticed he was being extra quiet, and thought she saw a little bit of his pattern starting, but she wasn't sure. She wanted desperately to give him the benefit of a doubt, and so she did.

Vernon had only been home a few minutes one night when Kelly asked, "Hey, Dad, can I borrow the car to go to the store to get a pack of cigarettes?"

Virginia thought better of it, but Vernon answered, "Sure, I don't care."

When Kelly had been gone a little longer than necessary, she told herself he must have run into someone and gotten caught up talking. But when Kelly had been gone well into the night, she couldn't lie to herself any longer. She knew what he had done, and that he had used their car to do it. She was just glad it was Friday night and she didn't have to work the next day. He would have to bring it back eventually.

*****

At the dope house, Kelly had tried to get fronted some cocaine, but the dealers wouldn't let him have it because he already owed them money again. It seemed like he was always in the red with them lately, but he needed his fix. He thought for a few minutes and with great reluctance said, "I'll let you hold the car until I bring you back the money." The dealers agreed to it and he gave them the keys.

After Kelly finished his supply, he called the police department and reported the car stolen. He retrieved the car, then went to another city and worked out the same agreement with another dealer. He finished his supply and called the car in stolen again. This time after he retrieved it he went home. He didn't think he could chance playing that trick again.

The next day Vernon kicked Kelly out of the house, just like he had many times before. He was beyond furious with what Kelly had done. He didn't know how to deal with his son, so he thought the best way was to just be rid of him.

*****

Kelly had gone to all of the counseling classes and Alcoholics Anonymous and Cocaine Anonymous and Narcotics Anonymous classes because they were court ordered. He had even helped set up the world dance for Cocaine Anonymous in 1988. But it seemed like nothing could get him on the right track. The programs helped him get clean for a few months, but nothing stuck. When life got hard, or the craving crept back, he would give in. He didn't know how to defeat it. He messed everyone over trying to meet his drug addiction need.

Kelly felt like things were finally going his way when he found some friends to stay with and even landed a roofing job. It didn't take long before his boss noticed that he was a good worker and that he excelled at making judgments and running crews, and so within a short time they promoted him to foreman. They gave him a company truck and he had a little more flexibility with his time. He was even able to do a shot of dope in between checking on jobsites.

Things were really looking up for him. He was doing work he really liked, he had a vehicle, and he could do the drugs as he wanted. He was sure he had finally found something he could do for a while. However, he couldn't keep up the façade for long. One day, well before the work day was up, Kelly had run out of drugs and decided to make a quick stop at the dealer's house. When he left he went to a motel to shoot up, instead of to the job site.

He woke up the next morning, never giving thought to the now-stolen truck he was in possession of. He drove just down the road from the hotel to see some friends at the taxi cab stand.

When he saw the police car pull up, he didn't think for a second that they were after him. He hadn't done anything lately to stir them up.

The two officers got out of their squad care and walked over to where Kelly and the taxi driver were talking. Without hesitation one of the officers asked, "Is this truck here yours?"

"No. It's a company truck." Kelly shrugged his shoulders. "And?"

"Well, it was reported stolen last night, and we found it with you. So I guess that means you're under arrest for unauthorized use of a motor vehicle. You're coming with us." As they proceeded to read him his Miranda rights and arrest him, Kelly tried to argue with them. He argued all of the way to the police station, and even after he was thrown into a cell.

The police kept him there for a few days before he went on to the Harris County Jail in Houston again. He dreaded calling his mom and telling her what happened. He knew she would be disappointed, and that his dad would act like he wasn't surprised. Vernon always said it was just a matter of time before

Kelly went to jail again, and that maybe the next time he would learn his lesson.

The only difference was that this time he wasn't in jail for drugs, but for the unauthorized use of a motor vehicle. He knew that since this was his third time down, the sentence was going to be harder, but he just wasn't sure how hard.

He hated the Harris County Jail. There was always a bunch of punk kids coming through thinking it was cool to be locked up, and worse than them were the jailhouse lawyers, who thought they knew everything but always got their clients the worst

> *The only difference was that this time he wasn't in jail for drugs, but for the unauthorized use of a motor vehicle.*

sentences. Then there were the people with jailhouse religion, who threw the Bible away on their way out. There wasn't anything cool about being in jail and having your freedom taken away, and the company inside left a lot to be desired.

Kelly couldn't get over how he had never seen this coming. He had thought that maybe he might end up back in prison for drug-related charges, but not for unauthorized use of a motor vehicle. That was crazy. He knew he had permission to drive that vehicle, but because he wasn't responsible with it, they had called it in stolen. That didn't make any sense to him. He couldn't figure out why they hadn't just taken the truck away and fired him. Kelly still was not taking responsibility for his actions, and now he was going to have to serve time again.

After the court hearing, Kelly thought he was going to die. The judge sentenced him to fourteen years with the opportunity at parole. Even in his most negative, worst-case-scenario thoughts, he had never thought they would give him such a long sentence. He didn't know how he could do almost fourteen years, but he also knew he didn't have any other choice.

CHAPTER
~ Twelve ~

No matter how hard Kelly tried or what he did, he couldn't make time go by faster. The days were endless and the weeks were eternity, but he was able to get in some college hours and more schooling on welding. Once he was moved to the Ramsey Unit in Rosharon, the wardens made him trustee and he was able to travel the prison farm, working on all of the welding. It helped with gaining experience and with passing time, but he learned that there would always be twenty-four hours in a day, and that they passed one at a time.

While at Ramsey, Kelly was also able to forge a good relationship with the guards. Since he had S1 trustee status and was the farm welder, he was able to travel about with liberty. He had more freedom there than he had on any other farm. He enjoyed riding the horses out to check on fences and finding repairs that needed to be made. He even crafted himself a fishing pole and got some fishing in, until the guards found out and made him stop. He was glad they didn't come down on him hard; they could have taken his privileges away, which would have made the time in prison unbearable. He was passing time the only way he knew how, and that was staying as busy as he could.

*****

He had petitioned the Board of Pardons and Paroles and been granted early release at the six-year mark. By the time he was set free in Huntsville he had served six consecutive years and still had eight years left of parole. The thought of having to report to a parole officer every month made Kelly cringe, but it was far better than having to serve out the eight years in prison. He would at least have his freedom back.

His main restriction was not being able to travel outside of the state line without a permit from the parole board, but he figured he could deal with that. It was a small limitation compared to prison time, where there was no freedom at all.

Coming home was different this time. Being gone for six years had a way of giving you a different perspective. So many people from his old life had changed, and he felt he barely knew them. Vernon had slowly been getting worse, and Virginia looked more stressed. Crystal had been helping carry the load of caring for their dad, and the guilt of not being around to support his family in their time of need weighed pretty heavy on Kelly.

Everyone treated him with kindness and acted like they were glad to see him, but he could tell there was some reserve. This had been his third time to prison, not counting the numerous times he had been to city and county jail. He was sure they were skeptical and didn't trust him, but did they have to make it so obvious? But in the end he didn't really care how everyone felt—he was just happy to be out and to be home. His main concern was that his mom was doing well, and everything else was secondary.

*****

Kelly spent a few months helping his mom around the house and getting reconnected with old friends. Since he had been gone, he learned of some who had overdosed and died, and others who were doing real badly because of the drugs. He didn't feel the camaraderie with them like he once had, and he thought that it was because of how long he had been away. No one had a good life, and they were all bums. He didn't see what he had ever had in common with them.

> *He knew the drug life wasn't desirable, but the craving for the drugs was always there.*

He knew the drug life wasn't desirable, but the craving for the drugs themselves was always there. His need had haunted him in his dreams during prison, and at night he would go through the motions of getting high over and over in his head. He felt as though no matter how hard he tried, he would never be able to escape the drugs.

*****

Virginia, who had never given up on her son, had somehow talked Kelly into going to church with her one Sunday morning. He had been out of prison for nine months, and she had been asking him for a while. She wasn't sure why he said yes, because she knew he was drugging again and that it was extremely bad this time, but she was glad he had agreed. Maybe this time would be the time when he allowed the Lord to touch his heart.

She had a responsibility for him that she couldn't explain. It went beyond a mother's burden. She knew God had plans for her son, but she just didn't know when Kelly would wake up and realize there was more to life than getting high. So far, he had always rejected God and turned to the drugs all of his life. But Virginia never gave up, because she knew the God that she served had His hand upon Kelly, and that gave her the hope to keep fighting.

Kelly knew that his mom really wanted him to go to church, especially since Brother Grimsley was there, and he had agreed because he couldn't explain the longing in his heart for something more. He didn't believe in all of that church stuff, and he truly felt they were lunatics and fanatics. But there was something deep inside of him that told him there was more to life than chasing a high to numb his pain. There had to be a way to heal the pain, not just cover it up. He knew he wanted life to change because the drugs had taken him farther into dissipation than ever before, but he didn't know how to live any other way. He had gone too far, and he felt there was no way to make things normal. And even if there was, he just wasn't sure he was ready for it yet.

*****

Kelly told his girlfriend, Debbie, that he was going to church with his mom. She could hardly believe it, but was glad he was going. All they had been doing lately was fighting. She decided to go with him, because she was tired of the way life was, too.

When he walked through the church doors, everyone greeted him warmly, although he wasn't sure why. He had long hair, a pack of cigarettes in his top shirt pocket, and wore a look that said, "I don't want anyone to talk to me."

He knew he had walls up, but the preaching stirred

something in his heart. When Brother Grimsley asked people to come to the front and pray, Kelly stayed in his seat. He didn't want any part of it. He thought Debbie was going to go for a minute, but then she remained beside him.

After a few minutes he saw Brother Grimsley approaching him; he felt cornered, not knowing where he could run. He didn't want to talk to the preacher; he didn't know what to say. When Brother Grimsley reached Kelly he put the microphone down and told him, "They would kill you if they could get to you, but they can't get to you because God won't let them." Then he went on to pray for someone else.

> *They would kill you if they could get to you, but they can't get to you because God won't let them.*

Kelly just sat there, stunned, not knowing what to say or do. He knew there were guys who were out to get him because he had taken some machine guns without paying, but he always thought that he was smart enough to stay out of their reach. Now Brother Grimsley had said that God was protecting him, but Kelly wasn't sure how to feel about that; he had never really believed in God and all that Bible stuff. He knew that God had spoken through Brother Grimsley, though. Debbie knew, too, and she sat beside Kelly, stunned, not sure how to respond.

*****

Everything was chaos after Sunday's service. Things were going horribly at work, and the fights with Debbie were worse than ever. Kelly had thought life was supposed to be better if you went to church, not worse. But what he didn't realize was that often things had to get worse before they got better.

When Virginia asked Kelly about going to church on

Wednesday night he went, partly because he wanted to be away from Debbie for the night, and partly because he was curious to see if Brother Grimsley had anything else to say to him.

There was an altar call again after service, and Kelly fought to stay in his seat and not go forward. He was so miserable and didn't see any way out of the drug addiction and lifestyle that went along with it. *I can't believe I am actually considering Jesus! What am I thinking? God can't help me.* His heart hardened, and he never made it to the altar.

The people had begun to disperse from around the altar and start back to their seats or to visit with other people when the pastor, Brother Nelson, came up to Kelly and said, "Let's go up front and pray, Kelly. Everyone is gone. I will go with you."

There was a moment of silence before Kelly replied reluctantly, "No. There will always be tomorrow. I can go tomorrow." They talked back and forth for a few minutes and Kelly refused to relent and pray.

He couldn't get out of the church building fast enough. He didn't want to go pray. What he had already heard about himself made him a little nervous, yet it also stirred something within him he couldn't quite explain. He still didn't see why God, if He did exist, would want anything to do with a sinner like Kelly.

*****

"Why don't you just get out and stay out?" Debbie was in a fighting mood. Kelly had only been with her for three months, but he knew it was time to break it off. He didn't care for her anyway—her house was really only a place to stay. The argument had started small, but now it had blown up and they were hollering at each other angrily. "You're never home anyway! And when you are home all you do is get high!"

He was throwing some of his clothes in a bag as he argued back. "Oh, like you never get high! I get you dope, too. So don't throw that at me. You're no angel! So don't even pretend. Stop lying to yourself and get over it, Debbie."

"Where are you gonna go, huh? Back to Momma's? Back to the motel where you were before?" she said with a sneer.

"That's none of your concern!" He threw the words back at her on his way out the door.

It was Friday, and he had just gotten off work and was barely through the door when he and Debbie had started arguing. He had just gotten paid and knew where he was going: to the dope house to get some crack. Once he learned that it was cheaper now than it used to be, and he could smoke cocaine instead of shooting it up, it was all he wanted. However, cheaper access had taken him down an even darker road over the last couple of months. It was hard for him to believe he had only been out of jail for nine months. It hadn't taken him long to get back on the drugs, and he fell harder and faster than ever before.

He spent his night in the hotel room, high and in total despair. The next morning he had a strange feeling and hid the rest of his rocks inside the edge of the box-spring mattress. He was still high when he heard a knock at the door.

"Who is it?" Kelly asked from inside the motel room. Fear had already started coursing through him.

"It's the narcotics officers. We need to talk to you."

Now Kelly was scared. He was glad he had hidden his stash. He just wished he would've hidden the pipe there, too. He put the pipe between both mattresses, but he knew that would be easy to find, and he didn't have time to move it because they might bust open the door and find him hiding it where his stash was. All of his thoughts began to race frantically.

As he opened the door he asked, "What do you want?"

The officers knew Kelly from the past, and they weren't going to waste any time in getting the handcuffs on him. They cuffed him as they answered him, "Your girlfriend said you stole her check, and we believe her."

Kelly couldn't believe it. Debbie was going to try and get him back for leaving without giving her any money. That was all she ever wanted: money. He had expected the cuffs right away, but not an accusation of stealing Debbie's check. "What money I have is mine. I work. I got it yesterday. I don't have her check. Man, I swear I don't. She's just mad at me 'cause I left her."

The police officers didn't argue with him; instead, they went on a search for it. Kelly knew they weren't going to find what they were looking for; he was just scared they were going to find something else. They already were familiar with his rap sheet and what he was known for. He tried his hardest to convince them to leave. They had just finished going through his bag whenever one of them went to the bed and flipped back the sheets. Then the officer lifted the mattress, and Kelly's heart sank when he pulled out the pipe.

"So, what's this? You still haven't cleaned your act up, Downing?"

"That's not mine, Officer." Kelly tried to play ignorant. "You know what this motel is known for. That could be anyone's who has stayed here before. It's not mine. I'm clean." Kelly wasn't sure how clean he looked because he was still high, but he continued to plead his innocence while they searched. They lifted the box spring, but when they didn't see anything right off they let it back down.

"Well, there's no check and no dope, but there is drug paraphernalia, and with your record, and this being your motel room, we're booking you and taking you in. You aren't getting outta this one."

Kelly pleaded with them. He knew where he was going. He was on parole, and with this arrest he would be considered to have violated it. He would be going back to prison, again. He hung his head as he sat in the Baytown City Jail while waiting for transportation to the Harris County Jail. He knew the inevitable was coming. He was so tired of the merry-go-round. He was ready to be done with it, but he just wasn't sure how. He had made a mess of his life.

He knew the inevitable was coming. He was so tired of the merry-go-round.

CHAPTER
~ *Thirteen* ~

At the Harris County Jail he went before the same judge he had seen many times before. She was known for issuing long prison terms, often the maximum that could be given. Kelly knew he was in for it.

The district attorney was just as bad as the judge. The D.A. glanced down at his file, looked at him long and hard, and then said, "Mr. Caywood, I see you are back. Mr. Caywood, you are a menace to society. You will never be anything but a drug addict. You will never amount to anything. Mr. Caywood, because of the laws of the state of Texas, I have to give you an attorney. But when you get your attorney and you come back, I am giving you a life sentence."

The judge backed the D.A. by saying, "I don't ever want to see you in my courtroom again." She slammed her gavel down and then said to the bailiff, "Get him out of my courtroom!"

The words "life sentence" went over and over in Kelly's mind. He didn't know how he was ever going to do life. He knew that with 134 misdemeanors and five felony convictions on his record he was going to do more time, but he had never expected a life sentence. The laws had just been changed to say that you

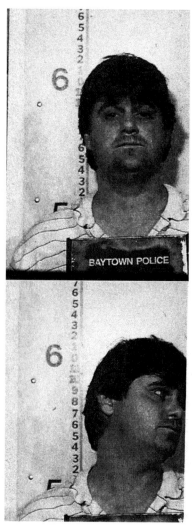

1998 Booking Picture

had to do thirty-five years on a life sentence before you had a chance at parole. And they only had him on drug paraphernalia! He couldn't believe what was going on.

He thought back to last Sunday; if he would have gone to the altar to pray he wouldn't have gotten busted three days later and received his fifth drug conviction. But of course, it was too late. Everything was too late. He was facing a life sentence, and he didn't stand a chance at any kind of life at all now. He began to wonder if the life in prison was better than the life on the streets in bondage to drugs.

The bailiff threw him in a holding cell with several other men, who looked to be in their early twenties. Kelly was thirty-three and didn't understand why he was getting put in this particular holding cell. When he asked the bailiff why he was there, he was told that the other cells were full. The young men resorted to calling him "Pops" because he was the oldest one in there.

On the way to his bed he passed a table with a paperback Bible sitting on it. Without a second thought, he picked up the Bible and went and knelt down in front of his bunk. He didn't care what anyone else saw or what they said. He knew he was desperate, and that this was the only hope he would have.

He prayed aloud, saying, "God, I know You are real, I just don't know how to get to You. I can't beat the drugs, the alcohol, or the cigarettes. If You are real like they say You are, You will help me this one last time. And if You help me this one last time, I will always tell someone what You did for me."

He opened the Bible to a random passage, and it was I Corinthians 10: 12-13: "Wherefore let him that thinketh he standeth take heed lest he fall. There hath no temptation taken you but such as is common to man: but God is faithful, who will not suffer you to be tempted above that ye are able; but will with the temptation also make a way to escape, that ye may be able to bear it."

The Word of God spoke to him. For the first time in his life Kelly felt like he didn't need anything else, that he could make it without the drugs and the alcohol—that he didn't have to live in bondage anymore.

He surrendered whole-heartedly to God and immediately began speaking in another language that was totally foreign to him. He couldn't control it or stop it. This wonderful experience felt better than any high he had ever known. He felt clean and pure and full of joy and peace. He had never felt anything like it before. He didn't want it to stop. He wanted to stay in this place forever. He knew he was in the presence of the Lord.

He had heard other people speak in tongues before, but he had thought they were all crazy. Now he knew it was real! God was real! Kelly knew this was the experience he had always heard of called the Holy Ghost, the spirit of God living inside of someone. He felt utter joy because God had chosen to fill him with His spirit!

He carried on speaking in tongues as the Spirit moved in him for several minutes. He wasn't sure how long he had been carrying on, but he knew he had scared the other men because they were banging on the door shouting, "Guards! Guards! This man's got a devil in him. You have to get him out of here." The guards never came, and eventually Kelly's cellmates calmed down when they realized he wasn't a threat.

For the first time in his life he felt peace. He knew that God would be his everything, and that he wouldn't want for anything. He fell asleep with the Bible beside him, still basking in the presence of the Lord and the new experience of receiving the Holy Ghost.

*****

Over the next few weeks, life had taken on a whole new meaning for Kelly. Gone were the fears, the doubts, and the insecurities. He was experiencing an inner peace he had never known before. It was what he had been searching for his whole life, but he had never known it until now. He had always thought people with this experience were lunatics and crazy. He thought they were just fanatical. Now it had happened to him! And he knew it was real!

> *For the first time in his life he felt peace. He knew that God would be his everything, and that he wouldn't want for anything.*

Although Kelly had gone to a Pentecostal church as a child, he still didn't understand everything that was going on. He knew he had received the Holy Ghost, but he didn't know how to explain it all. He immediately began praying, asking God to reveal to him the truths in His Word, and he started seeking for the answers in the Bible.

He decided the best place to begin was in the New Testament. He read Mark 16: 16-17, "He that believeth and is baptized shall be saved; but he that believeth not shall be damned. And these signs shall follow them that believe; In my name shall they cast out devils; they shall speak with new tongues." *So Jesus had spoken of people speaking in tongues before He was crucified.*

John 1:1, "In the beginning was the Word, and the Word was with God, and the Word was God." John 1:14, "And the Word was made flesh, and dwelt among us,..." If the Word is God, and the flesh was Jesus, then that means that Jesus was God in the flesh.

He found in John 3:3-7, "Jesus answered and said unto him, Verily, verily, I say unto thee, Except a man be born again, he cannot see the kingdom of God. Nicodemus saith unto him, How can a man be born when he is old? can he enter the second time into his mother's womb, and be born? Jesus answered, Verily, verily, I say unto thee, Except a man be born of water and of the Spirit, he cannot enter into the kingdom of God. That which is born of the flesh is flesh; and that which is born of the Spirit is spirit. Marvel not that I said unto thee, Ye must be born again."

He then understood that he had to be born again if he wanted to make it to Heaven. He couldn't make it just by believing. He had to act on that belief, and obey the rest of the Word of God.

John 14:26, "But the Comforter, which is the Holy Ghost..." Now he understood why, once he received the Holy Ghost, he had a peace and a comfort he had never known before.

Acts 2:3-4, "And there appeared unto them cloven tongues like as of fire, and it sat upon each of them. And they were all filled with the Holy Ghost, and began to speak with other tongues, as the Spirit gave them utterance." So before Jesus was crucified, He told them He was going to pour out His Spirit on them. Now, after He was crucified, He did. Once He filled them with His Spirit, they spoke with other tongues.

He went on to read in Act 2:12-13, "And they were all amazed, and were in doubt, saying one to another, What meaneth this? Others mocking said, These men are full of new wine." Acts 2:15-17, "For these are not drunken, as ye suppose, seeing it is but the third hour of the day. But this is that which was spoken by the prophet Joel; And it shall come to pass in the last days, saith God, I will pour out of my Spirit upon all flesh." I am not the only one that used the think they were crazy. Even people in the Bible days thought people speaking in tongues were drunk.

Act 2:37-41, "Now when they heard this, they were pricked in their heart, and said unto Peter and to the rest of the apostles, Men and brethren, what shall we do? Then Peter said unto them, Repent, and be baptized every one of you in the name of Jesus Christ for the remission of sins, and ye shall receive the gift of the Holy Ghost. For the promise is unto you, and to your children, and to all that are afar off, even as many as the Lord our God shall call. And with many other words did he testify and exhort, saying, Save yourselves from this untoward generation. Then they that gladly received his word were baptized: and the same day there were added unto them about three thousand souls."

All of the scripture began to come together in Kelly's mind and heart. To think that God would fill me with the gift of the Holy Ghost! With His Spirit! God loves me that much! And all I had to do was repent and surrender my life to Him. Oh, if only I would have done this years ago. I wouldn't have to carry the scars that I now carry.

It had only been a few weeks since he had received the gift of the Holy Ghost, but he felt like he was a totally different person. He continued to read the paperback Bible constantly, because he was so hungry for the Word of God. There was a deep longing for God within him, and the only source he knew to draw from was the Bible. When he had looked at the Bible before, it had seemed foreign to him. Now it was alive and it spoke to him. He understood it and wanted more and more of its wisdom.

He learned more about the mercy of God from II Corinthians 5:17, "Therefore if any man be in Christ, he is a new creature: old things are passed away; behold, all things are become new," and I John 1:9, "If we confess our sins, he is faithful and just to forgive us our sins, and to cleanse us from all unrighteousness." He knew that he had repented and that he was now a new creature in Christ. The old man was gone and he was now a new man. And he felt like a new man. His emotions, his thinking, it was all different. It was better. And He knew it was only the mercy of God.

The next set of scriptures that stayed with him was about fear. II Timothy 1:7, "For God hath not given us the spirit of fear; but of power, and of love, and of a sound mind," and I John 4:18, "There is no fear in love; but perfect love casteth out fear: because fear hath torment. He that feareth is not made perfect in love." He no longer had to live in fear. He was now able to live in the comfort of the Holy Ghost.

When other inmates would see him reading the Bible, they would want to debate. He knew he wasn't supposed to debate the Word of God because Truth is a defender of Truth, and the Word of God cannot come back void. It was at this time that the Lord lead him to II Timothy 2:23-24, "But foolish and unlearned questions avoid, knowing that they do gender strifes. And the servant of the Lord must not strive; but be gentle unto all men, apt to teach, patient."

Through it all, Kelly realized that there was scripture for everything that he faced in life. Although he didn't have anyone in jail to give him Bible studies, the Lord taught him through His Word.

*****

After a month of being in jail, one of the deputies by the name of Scott came to him and asked to speak with him. Once they were in the office, Deputy Scott said, "I know you are waiting for your court date, and may be waiting for a while, so I was wondering if you would like a job while you're waiting."

Kelly wasn't sure if he wanted a job. After being here so many times, he knew he didn't enjoy some of them. "What kind of job is it?"

"It's classifications. You'll be taking men from the

holding pod in the dungeon after they are processed in to the cells they are assigned to."

"How did you get my name?" Kelly asked. He had never heard of such a job before and couldn't figure out why they wanted him to do.

"I came into the office yesterday and saw 'Samuel Douglas Caywood aka Steven Kelly Downing' on my computer screen. I didn't think anything of it and pushed the 'delete' button. This morning I came back in and saw your name again on my computer, so I figured I would look at your record. You've been in a few times, waiting on a hearing now, and I needed a classification worker, so I thought you would fit. Do you want the job or not?"

"That's interesting how you got my name. Yeah, I'll take the job. Thank you." The only thing Kelly could think of was that he may be able to tell other people about Jesus and what He had done. He had told the Lord he would, and here was his opportunity.

When Kelly showed up the next morning, the deputy gave him a rundown of what he would be doing. Kelly thought he had everything figured out, then asked, "I'm going to be on that side of the glass, but where are you going to be?" He pointed to the bulletproof glass that separated the deputies from the inmates where he saw the inmates carrying on.

Deputy Scott chuckled and then replied, "I'm going to be at the desk on this side of the glass."

With shock, Kelly exclaimed, "You mean I am going to be out there telling all of the inmates where to go when I'm just an inmate like them!"

"Yep, that's what I'm saying," the deputy smirked.

The deputy had no further instructions for him, so Kelly walked out into the holding cell. There were over five hundred men in there, and he felt overwhelmed with what he had been commissioned to do. He realized he needed to have a little talk with Jesus. He walked to a small holding cell that was empty and

While taking the inmates to their cells, he had an opportunity to tell them about Jesus.

prayed. "Lord, I know I said I wanted to do something for You, but what do You want me to do with five hundred men?" He waited, then heard in that still small voice, "Speak to them one at a time." With assurance and peace Kelly left the room to do his job.

While taking the inmates to their cells he had an opportunity to tell them about Jesus. He told how he had lived a life addicted to drugs and how God had just delivered him and set him free and filled him with the Holy Ghost. He would then tell them of the new-found joy and peace that he had. They would often ask him to pray for them before he left to go back to the dungeon.

After a few weeks Kelly had started to gain favor with the guards. One morning when he walked in the atmosphere was tense. He decided to be a little bolder and asked, "Does anyone want to say a prayer?" He didn't expect much of a response and was surprised when sixty-six men stood up. He prayed for them as best he knew how, and the atmosphere in the room was transformed.

Eventually Kelly began saying the Lord's Prayer with them because it was the only prayer that didn't offend anyone or any religion. The number of men who wanted prayer grew every week. There were no more fights, and Kelly knew that it was because of God's calming presence in the place.

With Kelly always testifying about what God had done for him, the guards started asking him questions. They knew him from when he had come in before, so they knew there had been a change in his life. One of the guards approached him one day and said, "Kelly, you've been coming to this jail for a long time, and you're not the same as you used to be. You gotta tell me about this Holy Ghost and baptism in Jesus' name you're talking about."

This happened so many times over the next few months that Kelly lost count of the guards who came to him. He would tell them all he knew, and they were eager to listen and hungry for something different in their lives. He would call Brother Nelson and ask him about churches he could send them to. There was no time to dwell on the past, because he was so excited about what God was doing in the present.

CHAPTER
~ *Fourteen* ~

A small empty holding cell with a single desk and a few chairs had become one of Kelly's favorite places when he didn't have to put inmates into cells. He would sit and read his Bible for hours at a time. He had only been in the library for a few minutes when his mind went back to a conversation he had with Virginia a few months earlier.

"Now tell me what exactly happened again, Mom." There was no way he was hearing this correctly.

"There was a robbery at the Kroger grocery store here in Baytown."

"Yeah, I got that part," Kelly interrupted. He was trying not to be frustrated, but he wanted to hear the part again about what happened with Crystal.

"Crystal had just gotten off work from the hospital and was there to cash a check at the bank inside. She was at the teller station when the robbers walked in. One of them walked up to the teller station before anyone even knew what was going on." Virginia was trying to tell the story as best as she could, but Kelly was getting impatient.

"Okay, this is what I wanted to hear again."

"The robber put his pistol to her head and pulled the trigger, but when he pulled the trigger the clip fell out. While he bent down to grab the clip and put it back in the gun, Crystal ran and jumped behind a cash register."

"So she didn't get hurt?"

"No, but the robber turned and shot the teller behind the counter in the gut. Kelly, if the clip wouldn't have fallen out, then Crystal would be dead right now. This is horrible."

With relief that Crystal was okay he said, "Well, Mom, I just believe God had mercy on Crystal."

The old Kelly would have wanted to hurt the man who had put the gun to Crystal's head, even though he hadn't killed her. But Kelly knew God had taken out his stony heart and given him a fleshly heart just like Ezekiel 36:26 said. He knew the man's name and his family members' names, but he held no anger or bitterness against him. He had already forgiven the man in his heart.

A knock sounded at the door and a guard walked in with another man. Kelly knew this guard had been here for a long time and had seen Kelly come in again and again, but he hadn't been around Kelly this last time down, so he didn't know the change that had taken place.

The guard looked at Kelly and said, "Downing, take care of your business. He's all yours—I think you know who this is." Then he turned around walked back out the door. Kelly did know who it was—it was the man who had tried to murder Crystal. Not sure what was going on, the man came and sat in the chair across from Kelly. He looked to be in his twenties, which meant he still had his whole life ahead of him—but because of a stupid decision he'd made, he was going to spend most of the rest of his life behind bars.

Kelly understood what the guard meant. If Kelly wanted

to murder the man, he could, and get away with it. The guard knew Kelly's sister and the situation, and had already given him implicit permission. The man looked at Kelly as if he didn't have a care in the world and wanted to hurry up and get the meeting over with, because he had better things to do.

"Have you ever been to Baytown?" Kelly started the conversation out.

The man shrugged and said, "Man, I don't know what you're talkin' 'bout. I don't know nothin' 'bout no Baytown. You must be trippin' on somethin'. You don't know me."

"As a matter of fact, I do." Kelly then proceeded to tell the man his name, his mom's name, and some of the men who were with him the day of the robbery. Panic swept across the man's face and his eyes got big with fear. "That was my little sister's head you put the gun to in Kroger when the clip fell out." The man then began to cry.

> *Jesus Christ saved your life twice. I am not going to kill you. I want to pray for you.*

"Jesus Christ saved your life twice. The first time was when He died on Calvary for you, and the second time is right now, because I am not going to kill you. I want to pray for you." Then Kelly prayed for him. He knew the man was going to spend the rest of his life in jail for robbery and attempted murder, and he hoped that while inside this man could find God's grace, just as Kelly had.

*****

"What do you mean my attorney isn't showing up?" Kelly's patience was gone and he was angry. He had been in the Harris County Jail for nine months and had been waiting for his court hearing long enough. He knew God had worked things out with Mr. Cromwell, his attorney, because he took a post-dated check, but that didn't give him the right to miss the court hearing date. He had been waiting for hours in the courtroom holding cell. Brother Nelson had been outside of the courtroom praying for most of the day, too. Mr. Cromwell's absence was not how Kelly had planned for things to go today.

The guard was still standing there staring at Kelly and watching him vent. "Look, man, I don't have all of your answers. All I know is that they told me to come get you and send you back to your cell because something came up and your attorney isn't coming. So let's go, buddy."

There was nothing for Kelly to do but go back to his cell. The guard cuffed his wrists and ankles and told him he could go on through the long and confusing tunnels back to the jail. Just as Kelly was getting ready to walk out of the holding cell he saw an African American female inmate who looked to be about five feet tall, dressed in free-world clothes. Kelly thought it odd that she wasn't in a prison uniform like everyone else had on. As she passed, she paused, looked earnestly at Kelly, and said, "Just believe in Jesus."

Kelly's attitude was sour and his temper was flaring. "Yeah, I hear ya. 'Just believe in Jesus.' I am facing a life sentence and my lawyer doesn't show up. I don't have much faith right now. Whatever." Kelly's attitude was sarcastic, but he dismissed it all until he got to the end of the tunnel and turned around to look for the lady inmate. He didn't see her. He saw instead a few guards with two inmates, and asked them, "Where is that lady inmate? She was short and wearing free-world clothes."

The guard mocked him and said, "There was no lady inmate in that tunnel in free-world clothes." She laughed at him. "You need to get on across that tunnel, inmate. Stop stalling."

Kelly couldn't figure out what had just happened, but he didn't pay much attention because he was still upset about his situation. Once in the next holding cell in the jail, Kelly was given a bologna sandwich. He threw his paperwork down on a table and sat down. The other men around the table realized Kelly was upset and spread out.

A minute later Kelly felt a gentle hand on the middle of his back, and heard the lady's voice again: "Just believe in Jesus." Without a doubt, Kelly knew immediately that he had seen and heard an angel, and that God was trying to tell him to have faith and believe in Him. Gone were the fears, the doubts, and the anger. Kelly had an assurance that God would take care of him and would go before him and work things out.

The next day when Mr. Cromwell showed up, Kelly found out that he had gotten held up at another court hearing. After explaining the reason for the postponement, he wasted no time getting to business. "Okay, I just got back from the district attorney's office and I have all of your paperwork." He paused and added emphatically, "and you are going to like what I have to say. Your judge had to take a last-minute flight to Oklahoma last night. The D.A. is offering you time served. They are willing to take this charge from a felony conviction to a misdemeanor conviction."

Kelly was so excited he could hardly contain himself, "Man, it's Jesus. I know He worked it out. If I had seen the judge yesterday, I would have served out a life sentence. But she left last night and they're offering me time served today. It's a miracle from God!" He continued on in excitement and praising God for a minute until Mr. Cromwell decided he had waited long enough.

"So what are we going to do here, Mr. Caywood?" he said impatiently.

"Where's the paperwork for me to sign?"

Mr. Cromwell had a puzzled look on his face, then stood and said, "Hold on just a minute. Let me check on something." He left the room and then came back a few minutes later with paperwork in his hand. "They're not even asking you to plead guilty. I've never seen a case like this. This is incredible. You are one lucky guy."

...and you're still willing to drop this conviction from a felony to a misdemeanor and give him time served.

"God has given me favor. Now, I need to sign this paperwork before they change their minds."

When they went into the court room, the stand-in judge was looking over Kelly's booking records. He shook his head and then looked over at the district attorney. "District Attorney, have you looked at Mr. Caywood's record? He has five felony convictions and 134 misdemeanor convictions, and you're still willing to drop this conviction from a felony to a misdemeanor and give him time served after only serving nine months in county jail?"

The district attorney cleared her throat and said, "Yes, Your Honor, we've looked at his record. We've worked a deal out with Mr. Caywood, and this is what we are willing to do."

The judge thought for a minute and then said, "I don't understand it, but I'm going to approve it." Then he slammed his gavel down.

Kelly smiled and said, "Thank you, Your Honor, and District Attorney. I won't disappoint you this time." Then he turned and walked out with Mr. Cromwell.

"You're one very lucky man, Mr. Caywood. Yes, one very lucky man." They walked back to the office to finish up some paperwork. "That was the biggest hurdle to cross. But since you violated your parole, you also have to face the Board of Pardons and Paroles. You may still have to do some state time on a parole violation, but that is still much better than a life sentence."

Kelly agreed, "That is much better than a life sentence for sure. Let's just see what happens."

*****

Another month went by before Kelly heard anything back from the Board of Pardons and Paroles. They had voted to release him and let him return home, but the courts ruled to send him back to prison on his parole violation. The fact that the Board of Pardons and Paroles had voted for him to go home meant so much to Kelly, because it showed that they believed in him.

He had expected to be sent back to prison, but was still a little disappointed in the court's decision. Nonetheless, he decided to make the best of the situation. Although many people in prison believed that the Bible and religion was a crutch, Kelly was going to live God's Word in front of them, just as he had been doing since God had changed his life.

Huntsville had never been a place Kelly enjoyed. The authorities told him he was going to be there for two years, but he knew he needed to be somewhere else, and he believed God would provide another miracle. He knew he needed to learn more about the Word of God, and he wanted to be in a place where he could hear the truth taught. He also wanted to be close to home. Without delay he began praying that God would send him where he needed to be and yet still keep him close to home. After only a week the guards came and told him to gather his things, because he was being sent to another unit.

CHAPTER
~ *Fifteen* ~

The Duncan Unit in Diboll would be Kelly's new home. He was only two hours from Baytown, which showed that God had heard his prayer. In the church service held on Sunday, he realized that God had also answered his full prayer, not just part of it. There was an elderly man high-stepping down the middle of the chow hall saying, "In the name of Jesus. In the name of Jesus." When he preached, you could feel the anointing and the conviction of the Word of God. Kelly knew he was in the right place to learn more about the Bible, just as he had asked.

After the service he told the preacher who he was and that he had gone to a Pentecostal church growing up, and how God had delivered him from drugs. The preacher said, "Well, I believe God has had His hand on you for a long time, son. I am Brother Strong, and I pastor the Pentecostal church here in town. I am so glad to hear how God has delivered and set this captive free." They continued to talk for a few minutes until the inmates had to leave the chow hall and return to their cells.

Kelly still had not received the set-off letter from the parole department stating how long he would be down. He had been here for a while, and he knew he should have already heard from the parole board. When Kelly questioned the parole officer on the unit, he always said he hadn't received it.

This same parole officer at the Duncan Unit claimed to be religious, but did not show forth Christian character. Kelly had heard stories of how he would tie a little red ribbon around the set-off letters, hand them to an inmate, and say, "Merry Christmas, you still have twelve more months to do," with a big smile on his face, as if it brought him some kind of sick joy to tell the inmates they had to stay in prison longer.

When Kelly got the call to go to the officer's office, he had a feeling of how the scene was going to be played out, but wasn't sure exactly how long the set-off was. He sat down across from him and waited. The parole officer glared at Kelly, and then said, "Well, Mr. Caywood, looks like your set off has been here for a little while. I found it on the floor beside my desk." He chuckled. "I guess it fell off at some point and I just didn't see it." He picked up a rolled up paper with a red ribbon tied around it and handed it to Kelly. He said with pure glee in his voice, "Merry Christmas, Mr. Caywood, you have eighteen more months to do."

Kelly jumped out of his seat and started shouting, "Hallelujah, thank You, Jesus. Lord, You are good!"

The parole officer was caught off-guard and stopped Kelly in outrage. "Whoa, whoa, what are you doing? You have eighteen more months to do. Why are you shouting?"

Kelly smiled and laughed, "You don't understand. I only have eighteen more months, not eighteen more years! God has blessed me!"

It only took a few minutes before the parole officer grew tired of hearing Kelly shout praises to the Lord and asked him to leave.

Sundays brought excitement to Kelly because he always looked forward to hearing Brother Strong's preaching and being in the presence of the Lord. Brother Strong always preached with zeal and passion, and it brought conviction to their hearts. The teaching was so deep, and it fed Kelly's soul. He never would have thought that he would love the preaching and the Word of God so much. But God had made such drastic changes in his life that Kelly truly felt like a brand-new man.

There was always something to do to keep busy with. There were Bible studies he signed up for, and drug classes were offered periodically. A young man named Ken Cook taught one drug class, and Kelly learned that he was there as part of his training to be a juvenile probation officer. Ken had abused drugs in his past, but God had changed his life and filled him with the Holy Ghost. Ken told everyone that since he had received the Holy Ghost that he was a changed person, and he no longer needed the drugs to make him feel better. God had become his everything.

Kelly knew exactly what he was talking about and was so thankful to hear of someone else who had been delivered from drugs by the power of God. Though the class only lasted about a month, Kelly was glad to have created a friendship with someone who had lived the street life and had shared in the same experience as himself. He knew he would not forget the time spent with Ken.

Nothing could compare to the teaching and preaching Kelly received while on the Duncan Unit. His hunger for God deepened the more he learned, and he became close with Brother Strong, who was a solid minister of the Gospel that God had placed in Kelly's life at such a strategic time.

Just as Kelly thought he was going to be serving out his eighteen months and glean grace and wisdom from the blessed teachings, he received a letter from the Texas Department of Criminal Justice stating that he was going to be transferred to the Kyle New Visions Unit in San Marcos. He was disheartened about having to leave Brother Strong and being four hours away from home, but had to trust that God knew what was best.

Upon arriving at the Kyle New Visions Unit, Kelly found out that only first- and second-time offenders were sent there. He couldn't figure out how he, being a fourth-time offender, had ended up there. Only one in every forty-seven thousand inmates were transferred to Kyle New Visions, and it was considered by many to be a privilege. The Unit even offered rehabilitation programs, such as counseling and tools for substance abusers for when they were released. The program lasted for eighteen months—nine months at Kyle New Visions and nine months in a halfway house.

Kelly enjoyed the classes and learned as much as he could, but what he really liked were the church services and Chaplain McComb. Chaplain McComb worked at the facility and also pastored in a nearby town. Kelly was so thankful that the Lord had placed a strong man of God in his life once again.

After Kelly had been at Kyle New Visions for only a few months, the program director, Mr. Spencer, called Kelly into his office for a meeting. "How do you like being here?" he asked.

"I like it. It's much better than prison with no classes at all. The classes are important. I think everyone who's ever had a substance abuse problem needs to be a part of them." Kelly wasn't sure where Mr. Spencer was going, but he was glad to share his thoughts on the program.

"Well, Samuel, you show good leadership skills, and you have a good rapport with the men here. I would like to make you a cadre."

Kelly still got caught off guard when someone used his legal name, Samuel, but he had learned over the years to answer to it. It took a minute for him to register what the director had just said. "You want me to be a cadre? You mean you want me to teach the classes? To stand up in front of all of those men and teach the class?"

You show good leadership skills, and you have a good rapport with the men here. I would like to make you a cadre.

Mr. Spencer smiled, knowing Kelly hadn't been expecting this, and said, "Yes, that is exactly what I mean. I want you to teach the classes. About one in every one hundred and fifty thousand inmates has a chance to be a cadre. It's eight hours a day, five days a week. I've looked at your record. This is your fourth time down. And from what I've read, you're a different person than what you used to be. Your conduct here is impressive. I think you're the man for the job."

Totally astounded, Kelly said, "I appreciate the compliments, Mr. Spencer. I still can't believe you want me to teach, though. I have an outgoing personality, but when it comes to being in front of people and speaking, I am very shy. I've always been a nobody." Kelly paused. He knew God was showing him favor, and that He was preparing him for something. He felt truly blessed. He decided he was going to go through whatever door God was opening for him. After a minute Kelly looked Mr. Spencer in the eyes, "I would consider it an honor to be cadre and teach the classes to the men here. I'm sure I'll learn a lot in the process, as well."

"Good. I'm glad you made that decision. We'll do some training this week, and you'll start next week." They stood and shook hands before Kelly left the room.

He couldn't help but smile and walk a little taller with his head held high. Excitement about a new challenge and humility that he had been chosen were all emotions he felt coursing through him. On the way back to his bunk he passed Chaplain McComb.

"Someone looks happy!"

"I am a whole mixture of emotions. Mr. Spencer just asked me to be a cadre. I'm scared and excited and humbled all at the same time!" Kelly exclaimed.

"Congratulations!" Chaplain McComb patted him on the back. "That's great, buddy. I know God is just preparing you. He has great things in store for you. I know He does."

"Wow, thanks. I guess I'm still getting used to all of His blessings. I'm so humbled that He chose me and that He has blessed me so greatly. He's so amazing and just continues to blow my mind."

Chaplain McComb couldn't help but laugh, "Just wait. There's more. He's good at blowing people's mind." He continued to chuckle as he walked past Kelly to his office.

*****

The nine months of the program came and went, and Kelly was still there. He had gotten over his nervousness about teaching and was enjoying every minute of it, and he was learning much more by teaching the class than he would if he were only participating in it. While he was thankful for what God was doing, he knew it was time to move on. The nine months were up, and he was now supposed to move to a halfway house. He wasn't looking forward to going there, but he understood it was part of the program and there was no way around it. He had heard of a senator who had tried to get his son out of going to the halfway house, but was unsuccessful. Kelly figured that if a senator couldn't get his son out, then Kelly definitely couldn't petition the parole board and get out of it, either.

Another month went by and Kelly was still in San Marcos. No one had ever heard of anyone being in Kyle New Visions for ten months. Everyone who had come in at the same time as he had had already transitioned out. No one stayed past nine months—so what was Kelly still doing there?

While getting ready for church service on Sunday, Kelly was feeling frustrated. He had been able to talk to his mom more over the last few months and was ready to go home. Things were so different now, and he was ready to finally start living life. He knew it would take a while for his family to come around, but at least his mom knew how he had changed. In time, everyone would see what a different man he had become.

At the beginning of service Kelly said, "I am standing on the Word of God and believing that I am going to be at church with my mom next Sunday. Who will stand on the Word of God and pray with me?" A few men in the room stood with Kelly and began to pray. They believed God would provide the miracle.

Chaplain McComb preached about faith, and how sometimes we don't understand why things don't work out how we plan them, but that we have to trust God through it all, knowing He knows what's best for us. God was moving on Kelly during the whole service to just trust Him.

CHAPTER
~ Sixteen ~

August 2001

The next morning a guard came and banged on the wall and woke Kelly up. "Caywood! Caywood! Pack your stuff up. You're headed to Huntsville."

At first Kelly thought he was dreaming—he didn't know what to think. "What do you mean I'm headed to Huntsville? Why? What's going on?"

"I don't know what's going on. I just know you're going to Huntsville."

"Okay, thanks, man."

Kelly had just enough time to get his things together before being transferred. Kelly knew that this was a miracle all in itself. No one had ever been released to Huntsville, but only to a halfway house. This was unheard of, and he knew it was God's doing.

The drive was quiet on the way to the Walls Unit. Kelly still didn't know why he was going to Huntsville, so he decided to ask the sheriff's deputy. "Hey, deputy, you wouldn't happen to know why I am going to Huntsville, do you?"

The deputy transferred inmates all the time and didn't care much about conversation with them. But it was a simple question, and one he knew the answer to. He nonchalantly replied, "Yeah. You wrote a hot check a few years ago in Tyler, which is in Smith County, and it finally caught up with you in the system. So you have a detainer in Tyler, and they're supposed to come get you from Huntsville to take care of it."

"Are you serious! I have been in prison for two and a half years for a parole violation, and they're going to keep me from going home for a fifty-dollar detainer. That's ridiculous!" Kelly was furious that Smith County was doing this. They had access to his records. They knew how long he had served, which was more than enough time for a fifty-dollar detainer. They should have just given him a time served.

"That's all I know. As of right now, you don't have much say-so in the matter."

Kelly knew the deputy was right, but he still didn't like it.

On Wednesday Kelly was still at the Walls Unit and had not heard anything from Smith County. He was being held at the Golden Gates, where prisoners were released from. He hoped the Smith County authorities would just never show up, and then he could walk right through those gates and go home.

He was trying to be patient but was having a hard time at it. He asked the parole board at the Golden Gates, "Have y'all heard anything from Smith County? I've been here since Monday. I'm supposed to be at church with my mom on Sunday."

They disinterestedly replied, "Look, if they're not here by two o'clock tomorrow afternoon, we'll let you go and you'll just have to take care of it later with them. Just know that it's on your record until you get it taken care of."

That was relief to Kelly's ears. "Okay. Thanks. I appreciate it."

By noon on Thursday no one from Smith County had come to pick him up yet, and his hopes were high about going home. At one-thirty a guard came to his cell and said, "C'mon, Caywood, let's go." Kelly thought to himself, "Alright! I'm going home! I'm going home! I'm going home!"

If nothing changes, nothing changes.

He walked out of the cell and around the corner, headed out of the holding cell area. As he rounded the corner he saw a deputy, and his heart sank. The deputy looked at him and said, "Smith County Sherriff's Department, up against the wall." He proceeded to pat Kelly down and then put handcuffs and ankle cuffs on him for the drive to Tyler.

Kelly couldn't believe what was happening, but he had to believe that God had a reason for it all. He just wished he knew what it was.

After an hour on the road the deputy glanced at Kelly over his shoulder and asked, "So. What's your story?"

Kelly smiled. He just loved it when someone asked him his story. "Well, I'm glad you asked. I've spent my life addicted to drugs. I used to do sixty shots of cocaine a day. I've been to prison four times. I have 134 misdemeanors and five felony convictions. While in jail God filled me with the Holy Ghost. I went from a life sentence to one year in the county jail, time served. I'm a four-time loser, but a lifetime winner in Jesus Christ. If nothing changes, nothing changes." He stopped talking when the deputy started to pull over on the side of the road.

The deputy turned around to face Kelly. "Man, I have never seen anyone like you. Are you serious? Did you really used to be a druggy and now you are trying to live for God?"

"Yes, it's all true."

"Wow. That's incredible. Look, I know you've been in jail this last time for two and a half years, and now they have you going to Tyler for a fifty-dollar detainer. If there's anything I can do to help with this process, I will."

"Anything you can do would be fantastic. I am supposed to be at church with my mom on Sunday."

The deputy shook his head, "I'm sorry, but I don't think that's going to happen. Your judge is going to be out of town until Monday. There's no one you can see."

"Oh no. Do we have any other option?"

"I don't know. Let me think about it."

He pulled back onto the road and was quiet for a little while. They chatted some and then the deputy made a few phone calls.

When they arrived at the jail, the deputy asked Kelly, "Do you think you can get some money to make a bond?"

Kelly thought a minute. "Yeah, I think so. I can probably get some from my little sister, Crystal. How much do you think I'll need?"

"They will let you go on a three hundred dollar bond."

"That would be awesome. Can I call her now?"

"You bet." He pointed to a phone across the room. "You can use that phone."

Kelly called Crystal and explained to her what was going on. Crystal said that she and Virginia could be there that evening with the money. As soon as Kelly got off the phone with her, the deputy walked back into the office.

"Do you think you can call your sister back?"

Kelly got nervous and wasn't sure how to answer. With uncertainty he said, "Yes. Why?"

"Well, I was able to find a judge who is willing to come in tomorrow just to hear your case if you are willing to stay in jail one more night and go from cell to cell and tell the other inmates what God has done in your life."

Kelly's jaw dropped. This situation just kept getting more interesting. "Of course I will stay for another night to tell them what God has done."

"Good luck, buddy. I won't be here tomorrow because I am off. It was nice meeting you. I wish you the best."

"Thank you for everything. I appreciate all you have done." They talked for a few minutes and then Kelly called Crystal back and told them not to come until the next day.

After spending the night in jail and going from cell to cell, he was finally able to go home. God had performed the miracle and answered his prayer. He was going to be at church with his mom on Sunday.

If Kelly had been released from Huntsville, they would have given him clothes to change into instead of having him leave in his prison whites. But county jails didn't offer clothes for inmates to change into. He had never heard of anyone leaving in their prison whites, yet he was about to. It was just another sign that God's hand was on his life.

When Kelly walked out of the jail he looked over to his right side and saw the deputy standing there. "I thought you were off today. What are you doing here?"

The deputy walked over to him. "I just had to come see you one more time." They shook hands and said their goodbyes one more time before Kelly walked to where Virginia was waiting for her son.

CHAPTER
~ *Seventeen* ~

Church was a whole new experience for Kelly. Although he had been to worship services many times in the past, his experiences in prison had changed him. Gone was his rebellion against Christ, and in its place stood the love of a Savior. Brother Nelson preached with fervency and zeal. It convicted the very core of Kelly's soul and encouraged him to live for God harder than ever before.

The idea of finding love was far from Kelly's mind, but on the second row he saw a young lady worshipping God with all of her heart. The sincerity with which she loved the Lord and greeted those around her stirred something within him, and he knew she would be the woman he would one day marry.

That Sunday morning he met many people in the congregation who would be his new church family. The joy of being around people who showed him love and acceptance met him with deep appreciation for how God had drastically changed his life.

He inquired about the young lady and many people told him she had just moved from Louisiana that weekend, and that her brother had been going to church here for a while. Without even speaking to her, he knew what he felt. He was bold enough to tell Virginia and a few other people that she was going to be his wife.

Before Kelly and Virginia left, Brother Nelson came and talked to them for a few minutes. He asked Kelly how he had enjoyed service and then questioned, "Did you know that there was going to be some animosity toward you from your family because you're coming to church here?"

Kelly was a little surprised, but not totally caught off-guard. "No. I didn't think it was going to be a problem, but I used to be a mean man. They don't trust me. I've claimed to have straightened up in the past, but I never stuck with it."

"You're right. They don't trust you. Before you even came here a few members of the congregation told me that they weren't going to come to church here anymore if you walked through those doors. They think you're going to relapse and take advantage of everyone. They said you've never stayed clean very long."

"Well, I'm sorry they feel that way. I did try to straighten up before, but I fell and I did take advantage of them. I would like them to trust me, but I guess I am just going to have to prove myself. I'm sure they will see the change in time, and that I am not the man I used to be."

Brother Nelson knew that Kelly was not the same man. He knew the power of God to deliver people and change people's lives. He smiled and said, "I'm sure they will." He patted Kelly on the back. "I'm sure they will. I will see you tonight."

"Yes sir. I will be here."

Virginia was disappointed when they got in the car to go home. She was excited because she knew her son was different. He had been living for God for two and a half years now, and she knew he was for real this time. But no one else in the family believed it, and she was frustrated that they couldn't see Kelly as he was now—instead, they focused on the man he used to be. She succumbed to playing the waiting game, because she had faith that it was only a matter of time before everyone they knew would realize the complete change that had taken place in Kelly's life.

*****

Kelly had no trouble keeping busy now that he had been released from prison. It had only been a few months since he had been home, and already God had blessed him with many godly friends and a good welding job. He often found himself overwhelmed with thankfulness at all God had done in such a short period of time, and he frequently lifted his thoughts up in prayer and thanks.

Although everyone in the church knew that Kelly loved the Lord and was faithful, some of his family still had a hard time believing it. He recently heard one say, "It's only been a few months. Give him ninety more days. Kelly has never been clean for three months." When Brother Nelson gave him a key to the church, some members of the congregation were worried he would steal everything the church had. He didn't know how much longer it was going to take to convince them otherwise, but he was going to keep living the Christian life in front of them anyway.

Within the next couple of months his family slowly started to acknowledge his true change. The ones who said they wouldn't have anything to do with the church if Kelly joined the congregation were now saying, "Kelly got something in that prison. He really got something." And the ones who had stopped serving God or had never served Him before said, "Kelly got something in the jail, and I want to know what it is. He's never been clean this long. Whatever he got was real, and I want it."

Over the next several months Kelly saw more and more family members come to church and begin to

God had restored the many relationships Kelly's drug addiction had broken.

faithfully serve the Lord. He prayed with them, cried with them, and laughed with them. He grew closer to his family more than he ever had before. He was finally starting to learn what family meant. God had restored the many relationships Kelly's drug addiction had broken.

*****

January 2002

Things kept getting better for Kelly, and now there was a new turn in his life. He had finally started a relationship with the lady in the second row, who he now knew was Barbara Clark. The relationship bloomed quickly, and they were soon falling in love.

Kelly and Barbara were engaged by March and he was more ecstatic than ever before. God had provided for him abundantly in so many ways. He was blessed with friends, with a job, with a home of his own, and with the restoration of relationships with his family, and now he was going to be blessed with a wife.

Come July he would be a very happily married man. The woman he would spend the rest of his life with shared the same love for God and for reaching people as he did. He could never have thought that within a year his life would become so fulfilling, but he was grateful to the Lord that it had.

*****

July 2004

Despite all the blessings in Kelly's life, there was also sorrow. Vernon's multiple sclerosis had taken almost twenty years to deteriorate his body, but he was now at the point of being close to death. His body was shutting down, hospice was called in, and the family was told to stay close.

Although there were past events that Kelly could have used as an excuse to stay away from his dad, he didn't. Over the last two years Kelly, Barbara, and Virginia had taken care of Vernon and seen to his needs. Kelly and Vernon's relationship was not as good as a father-son relationship should be, but there were no more harsh words. The anger had been replaced with real communication.

Vernon's wishes were that he pass away at home and not in a hospital. During his last week, he quietly slipped into a coma, and the family did all they could to keep him comfortable. Since welding jobs had been harder to come by close to home, Kelly was drawing unemployment and was thankful for the time he was able to be with his family.

After four days of being in the coma Vernon woke up. He didn't have any motor skills, but he could talk a little and knew what was going on around him. Kelly needed some closure and asked to have a few minutes alone with his dad.

Once everyone left the room, Kelly sat down on the chair next to Vernon. He took Vernon's hand and held it between his. With sorrowful emotion in his voice he said, "Dad, I'm sorry I haven't been the son you wanted me to be. I'm sorry for all of the years I caused pain for you and Mom. I promise I will take care of Mom when you pass. She won't do without. I will take care of her." He paused, and said something he hadn't said for a very long time. "I love you, Dad."

A single tear rolled from the corner of one of Vernon's eyes. He squeezed Kelly's hand and then said in a barely audible voice, "I love you, too, son."

Kelly broke down crying. He had never heard his dad say those words. He was sad that it had taken so many years, but thankful to God that he was able to have the closure he needed, and the healing that went along with it.

Vernon went back to sleep a few hours later and never woke up again. He passed away the next day with family surrounding him. While it was a sad time, peace and comfort surrounded the family, because they knew the Author and Finisher of their lives.

*****

The economy had slowed some in the welding and pipefitting industry around the Houston area, and there were not many jobs. The short turnaround jobs Kelly was able to find were all out of town, and he knew he needed to be home. He had been praying about starting a roofing and construction company of his own, because he was familiar with the trade and he was good at it.

He decided to go for it, and within a few weeks Kelly landed his first client. The job consisted of replacing the roof, fascia, and soffit on a house. He immediately got a DBA with K&B Construction, owners Kelly and Barbara Caywood.

He felt God's hand upon their lives and the construction company and knew that if he was faithful to the house of God and the principles of God, that they were going to be blessed. Little did he know just how much God was going to bless them, and how much of a blessing they were going to be to others.

*****

In the spring of 2006 Kelly walked into the church on a Sunday morning expecting Brother Nelson to be preaching, but instead had a much-welcomed surprise. He saw Ken Cook in the sanctuary greeting people before service, and it was Ken who would preach the service that day.

Kelly walked up to Brother Cook and introduced himself again to him. Brother Cook instantly knew who he was and excitedly gave him a hug.

When Kelly stepped out of the hug he asked, "What are you doing here? I never thought I would see you again."

Brother Cook laughed and then replied, "I never expected to see you either. My wife and I are evangelizing now, and God has opened the door for us to be here."

"Wow!" Kelly exclaimed. "Incredible! Let's please keep in touch."

"Let's do. Let's stay in contact with each other."

Brother Cook held many evangelistic services over the next month and their friendship quickly grew. True to their word, they stayed in contact with each other and remained close friends. God has blessed their times together and each of their ministries.

*****

Shortly after meeting Ken Cook, Kelly was introduced to one of his greatest mentors, Charles Mahaney. Brother Mahaney was from the same background as Kelly. He was the General Chaplain of the Christian Prisoner Fellowship and traveled the nation evangelizing and preaching the Gospel. Brother Mahaney spoke into Kelly's life and imparted deep teachings

> *For the first time in his life, since he was eleven years old...he was no longer a ward of the State of Texas.*

to him. He had a profound effect on Kelly's life. In the year they were able to spend together, before Brother Mahaney's passing, he helped birth a burden within Kelly that set the course that Jesus would later lead him down.

*****

Kelly was faithful to the house of God and served in every capacity he could. He enjoyed working in the kingdom of God. He worked in many different departments in the church— Sunday School teacher, youth leader, hospitality, prison ministry, drug classes, Bible studies, coordinated outreach, leading services, hospital visitation, and preaching. He was never scared to be involved and considered it a privilege.

In the spring of 2008, there were two major happenings in Kelly's life. He was finally released from parole on April 23, 2008. For the first time in his life, since he was eleven years old and went to the Harris County Youth Village, he was no longer a ward of the State of Texas. He had his complete freedom from the judicial system.

The next month Kelly received his ministerial license with the United Pentecostal Church, International. In the following year, the spring of 2009, Kelly and Barbara both knew God was calling them to evangelize. With the economy becoming increasingly unstable and some of their major construction contracts starting to close, they were not sure what direction they should go. Along with their uncertainty of vocation, Brother Nelson was also retiring as pastor of the First United Pentecostal Church in Mont Belvieu.

Kelly had never preached a revival, but the burden and passion for evangelism burned deep within him and drew him to his knees in prayer for direction from God. After much prayer and fasting, he knew without a doubt that he was being called to evangelize. He wasn't sure how everything was going to work out, but he trusted the Lord.

He also knew that with Brother Nelson retiring, God was moving him on to another place and another pastor, but wasn't sure where that was going to be, either. On a Friday afternoon Kelly and Barbara went to the church to talk to Brother Nelson about everything God had been dealing with them about.

After talking, Brother Nelson laid hands on them both, prayed over them, and released them into the hands of the Lord. He gave them his blessings and said he would be praying for them. The next day Kelly received a call to preach his first revival.

While praying about where to go to church and which pastor should be their watchman on the wall, Kelly clearly heard the voice of the Lord leading him to the Apostolic Temple in Pasadena, Texas, pastored by Brother McClain. The moment they entered the sanctuary they knew this would be their new home. And when Brother McClain said from the pulpit, "If I can't weep for your soul, then I can't pastor you," they knew God had blessed them with a new pastor.

EPILOGUE

After Kelly preached that first revival, God continued to open the doors for him and Barbara to evangelize. Although Kelly expected to be able to operate K&B Construction and preach the Lord's Word, God had other plans. He wanted Kelly and Barbara to trust in Him and depend on Him completely. Therefore, the Caywoods closed the doors on K&B Construction and discontinued operating it.

They sold their home and their furnishings and now travel the nation, preaching the Gospel everywhere they go. God has blessed them and opened many doors of opportunity to evangelize. They have witnessed the salvation of the Lord and the many miracles He has performed. God continues to do great and mighty things, and there is still much, much more to come. With God's grace, all things are possible—and Kelly's story is a shining example of that truth.

To God be all of the glory!

2009 Africa Crusade
Over 1,200 people received the gift of the Holy Ghost

Kelly and Barbara after service

Kelly & Barbara at San Jacinto Battleship

ABOUT THE AUTHOR

Rev. Kelly Caywood is a licensed minister with the United Pentecostal Church, International. He and wife, Barbara Caywood, travel full time doing the work of an evangelist. While they are from Baytown, Texas, they make their home wherever the call of God takes them. They live out a life of passion after the heartbeat of Jesus Christ. Their true joy comes from witnessing the power of God changing lives. To them, nothing is a sacrifice, but it is their reasonable service.